RHYTHM
IN SEVENTEENTH-CENTURY
ITALIAN MONODY

RHYTHM
IN SEVENTEENTH-CENTURY ITALIAN MONODY

WITH AN ANTHOLOGY
OF SONGS AND DANCES

PUTNAM ALDRICH

W · W · NORTON & COMPANY · INC · NEW YORK

FIRST EDITION

Library of Congress Catalog Card No. 64-13989

Published simultaneously in the Dominion of
Canada by George J. McLeod Limited, Toronto

FOR THE PUBLISHERS BY THE VAIL-BALLOU PRESS, INC.
PRINTED IN THE UNITED STATES OF AMERICA

1 2 3 4 5 6 7 8 9 0

CONTENTS

PREFACE

THIS BOOK IS THE CONSEQUENCE OF THE AUTHOR'S ATTEMPT TO SOLVE CERTAIN rhythmic problems encountered in the transcription of seventeenth-century music for present-day use.

Musical notation, in the seventeenth century, was in a state of transition. Its signs and symbols, inherited from the older mensural system, were no longer used in the same way that they were during the Renaissance but had not yet acquired the significance that we attribute to them today. It appeared that the best way to determine the composers' intentions would be to examine and compare a large number of original manuscripts and prints of the period. This required a year of research in Italian libraries, which was made possible by a Guggenheim Fellowship and a grant from the Fulbright Commission.

Even the original sources, however, failed to furnish conclusive evidence for the solution of some of the problems of notation. Since these were chiefly problems of rhythm and meter, and since much of the music in question was intended to be sung and danced, as well as played on instruments, I undertook an intensive study of the Italian verse meters and dance movements that were cultivated in the early seventeenth century. The close relationship between the rhythms of music, poetry, and dance provided clues to practically all the cases in which the musical notation is obscure or ambiguous.

With the cooperation of Elizabeth Hunter Morrill, an American singer residing in Florence, I was able to test the results of my investigations in actual musical performance and at the same time to bring to light a repertoire of attractive music that has been totally neglected since the seventeenth century.

RHYTHM
IN SEVENTEENTH-CENTURY
ITALIAN MONODY

ONE

THE PROBLEM

Musical Performance and Musical Notation

THE TWENTIETH-CENTURY REVIVAL OF BAROQUE MUSIC HAS PROVIDED AN impetus toward the reconstruction of many of its outward aspects: the tone of the harpsichord, viols, and recorders; the correct reading of symbols for ornaments; the realization of figured basses, etc. Very little has been done, however, in the way of reviving the original performance style of this music. What we hear, in all too many current renditions of Baroque music, is either a watered-down Romantic style or else an accurate, but dry and lifeless, reading of the notes. A vibrant performance of any type of music is contingent upon the recognition and projection of its inner qualities. Foremost among these are the rhythms intended by the composer, and these are precisely the qualities that are the hardest to discover through the inadequate symbols of musical notation. Only by finding the missing links between the written notes and the living rhythms they once symbolized can we arrive at a means of making the revival of Baroque music a resuscitation rather than a mere reconstruction. Every sensitive performer realizes, of course, that this is the most crucial as well as the most difficult problem in the interpretation of the music of *any* period. It is especially difficult, however, in the case of seventeenth-century music because of the graphic form in which it has come down to us.

The musical notation of the seventeenth century, as contrasted with that of the Middle Ages and the Renaissance, bears so close a resemblance to our own that the differences in meaning of its symbols are constantly overlooked, with the result that many (if not most) modern editions of this music present it in a distorted form that misrepresents the intentions of the composer. The new developments in musical style that took place in Italy around the beginning of the seventeenth century were reflected in the notation. New symbols were introduced—barlines, new time signatures, figured basses, tempo indications. The transition from the old mensural notation to "metrical" notation, however, was not a sudden but a gradual one. Many features of the older system remained in force much longer than is generally believed, and many of the innovations did not yet have the significance we attribute to them today. One of the main problems for the transcriber of this music is that of determining the state of musical notation at the time and place of origin of a given manuscript or print. Musicologists and editors have occasionally been forced to recognize the existence of such problems when they have come across passages that simply do not make musical sense when transcribed in the conventional manner. They have attacked them, and have sometimes arrived at satisfactory solutions for isolated cases.[1] But up to the present no scholar has made an adequate investigation into the various and successive phases of musical notation during the seventeenth century.

This essay does not pretend to solve all the problems of rhythmic interpretation of seventeenth-century music; the field is obviously far too vast to be treated in a short study. But one must begin somewhere, and it seems preferable to start with an intensive study of a restricted period and style rather than to attempt a necessarily superficial survey of a larger area. There is no doubt that Italy was the dominant musical influence throughout Europe in the early years of the century and that many features of the international Baroque style have their roots in the music of the Italian monodists. Much of this music is inextricably bound up with words or dance, or both. In our study of musical rhythms we shall therefore be able to make constant cross-references to their counterparts in poetic and dance rhythms. In cases where the musical notation itself is too vague or too ambiguous to warrant conclusive interpretations, we may have recourse to the corresponding rhythms of verse or dance.

Poetry, Music, and Dance in the Early Seventeenth Century

Two distinct types of rhythm were cultivated by the composers and performers of the Baroque era: a free rhythm in which the steady beat of the

1. Specific instances of problematic notation are discussed in the following articles: W. Apel, "Anent a Ritornello in Monteverdi's *Orfeo*," *Musica Disciplina*, V (1951), 213ff.; Fritz Noske, "Two Problems in Seventeenth-Century Notation," *Acta Musicologica*, XXVII, fasc. iii–iv (1955); Arthur Mendel, Review of *The Lost Tradition* by Fritz Rothschild, *The Musical Quarterly*, XXXIX (1953), 611ff.; Arthur Mendel, "A Brief Note on Triple Proportions in Schütz," *The Musical Quarterly*, XLVI (1960), 67.

Renaissance was abandoned in favor of a flexible disregard for strict tempo (described by Giulio Caccini as "that noble manner of singing with *sprezzatura*"),[2] and a strict rhythm based upon more or less stereotyped patterns derived from dance movements or from poetic meters. Both types appear in the earliest publications of the monodists: in Caccini's *Le Nuove Musiche* of 1602, for instance, *Amarilli mia bella* is an example of the first, and *Udite, udite amanti* of the second. Both types, moreover, continue to exist side by side throughout the entire Baroque period and are often coupled in contrasting pairs, as in the recitative and aria of Neapolitan opera and in the toccata and fugue of the early eighteenth century. It is the second type, however, that is most characteristic of the greater part of Baroque music; identical dance-like patterns occur again and again, treated in diverse ways by different composers and in different kinds of pieces. Some of them become associated with specific "affections" and thus, according to the aesthetic doctrine of Baroque musicians, determine the expressive character of the particular piece or movement in which they are used. The performers of the time, recognizing through the rhythmic pattern the affection intended by the composer, were enabled to give to the music its appropriate tempo, accentuation, phrasing, and articulation—all those elements of expressive execution that are carefully indicated in later music but for which directions are notably lacking in Baroque scores.

By the year 1630 many of the dance-like patterns that were to become ingredients of later Baroque composition had already crystallized in the voluminous output of music for intermezzi, balli, carnevali and other entertainments, by composers attached to Italian courts. These compositions, though mostly occasional pieces in the sense that they were originally created for immediate use at specific court functions, were nevertheless widely circulated both in prints and manuscripts. They must be regarded as representative of the main stream of Italian secular music during the early part of the century, when the production of opera was still a rare and specialized occurrence and the cantata had not yet assumed its standard form and importance in the musical repertoire.

The pieces in question were entitled, more or less indiscriminately, "Aria," "Canzonetta," "Scherzo," "Ballo," "Balletto," or even "Madrigale." Often they were grouped together in collections called simply "Musiche." The musical source material for this study is contained in the following prints

---

2. G. Caccini, Foreword to *Le Nuove Musiche*, 1602, passim. Translation in O. Strunk, *Source Readings in Music History*, N.Y., 1950, pp. 377ff.

and manuscripts, which will hereafter be referred to by the composer's last name as shown in the right-hand column.

Giulio Caccini—*Le Nuove Musiche*, Florence, 1602	CACCINI, 1602
Cesare Negri—*Nuovi Inventioni di Balli*, Milan, 1604	NEGRI
Jacopo Peri—*Varie Musiche*, Florence, 1609	PERI
Hercole Porta—*Hore di Recreatione Musicale*, Venice, 1612	PORTA
Tomaso Cecchino—*Amorosi Concetti*, Venice, 1612	CECCHINO
Pietro Pace—*Primo Libro di Madrigali*, Venice, 1613	PACE
Antonio Brunelli—*Scherzi, Arie, Canzonette e Madrigali a una, due, e tre voce, Libro Secondo*, Venice, 1614	BRUNELLI, 1614
Raffaello Rontani—*Le Varie Musiche a 1, 2, e 3 voce*, Florence, 1614	RONTANI
Giulio Caccini—*Nuove Musiche e Nuova Maniera di Scriverle*, Florence, 1614	CACCINI, 1614
Marco da Gagliano—*Musiche a due e tre voci*, Venice, 1615	M. GAGLIANO
Domenico Visconti—*Il Primo Libro di Arie a una e due voci*, Venice, 1616	VISCONTI
Antonio Brunelli—*Scherzi, Arie, Canzonette e Madrigali, Libro Terzo*, Venice, 1616	BRUNELLI, 1616
Filippo Vitali—*Musiche a due, tre e sei voci*, Florence, 1617	VITALI
Vincenzo Calestani—*Madrigali et Arie Per Sonare e Cantare*, Venice, 1617	CALESTANI
Lorenzo Allegri—*Il Primo Libro delle Musiche*, Venice, 1618	ALLEGRI
Giovan Batista da Gagliano—*Varie Musiche, Libro Primo*, Venice, 1623	G. B. GAGLIANO
Alessandro Capece—*Il Secondo Libro de Madrigali et Arie*, Rome, 1625	CAPECE
Pietro Bucchianti—*Arie, Scherzi e Madrigali*, Venice, 1627	BUCCHIANTI
Pietro Paolo Sab[b]atini—*Il Sesto. Opera Ottava*, Rome, 1628	SABBATINI

Martino Pesenti—*Il Quarto Libro de Madrigali*, Venice, 1638	PESENTI
Gasparo Zanetti—*Il Scolaro*, Milan, 1645	ZANETTI
MS *Barbera*—in the possession of Professor A. Damerini, at the Conservatorio L. Cherubini, Florence	BARBERA
MSS *Magliabecchiana XIX*, *25*, *66*, and *115*—at the Biblioteca Nazionale Centrale, Florence	MAGL. XIX, 25 MAGL. XIX, 66 MAGL. XIX, 115

The pieces are mostly syllabic settings of strophic songs in strict verse forms. Many of them were intended to be danced and played on instruments as well as sung. They therefore constitute a particularly rich field for the study of relationships between music, poetry, and dance. It is often possible to compare expressions of the same rhythm through musical tones, poetic meters, and dance movements. Such comparisons reveal several very significant facts. One is that a close analogy exists between the musical setting of a strict verse form and the composition of a tune to accompany a specific pattern of dance steps. Both require rhythmic units of prescribed lengths with caesuras, climaxes, and pauses at predetermined moments. In the case of some dance songs one cannot guess which was conceived first—the dance, the poetry, or the music. In other cases, composers like Brunelli and Pesenti show us precisely how the rhythm of a given melody can be adjusted to fit a gagliarda or a corrente.

Another significant fact is that identical rhythms are frequently expressed in different notations. Musical notation was clearly in a transitional stage. There was no single accepted manner of notating a specific rhythm, and composers were given to experimenting with various ways of trying to make their intentions clear. Time signatures in the notation of this period do not have the same implications that they have in later music; neither do they have quite the same proportional significance that they had in the sixteenth century. Barlines are often entirely absent. When they do occur they are used to measure off regular units of time corresponding to the duration of the *tactus*. Practically never do they have the metrical connotations that they have today.

In view of these discrepancies, it is evident that to talk about these rhythms in terms of one or another of the ways in which they have been notated would only lead to confusion. The primary requisite for any meaningful discussion of musical rhythms of another period is obviously a terminology that deals with rhythm independently of its notation. Unfortunately there is no such terminology that has anything like general acceptance. It therefore seems advisable to preface this study with definitions of terms in the senses in which they will be used throughout. This preface will at the same time constitute a short disquisition on:

The Nature of Musical Rhythm

In the first place we should recognize, as did the ancient Greeks, that rhythm is an activity, not a thing. Aristoxenos distinguishes between *rhythmos*, the act of rhythming, and *rhythmizomenon*, the thing rhythmed; the latter, he says, may consist of verse syllables, bodily movements, or musical tones.[3] In the case of Western music the *rhythmizomenon*—the thing to be rhythmed—is meter. Meter is an organization of temporal durations that I shall define in terms of pulses, beats, and measures.

Pulses are those regularly recurring impulses that must be organized to form metric units, for pulses in themselves are undifferentiated and metrically neutral, like the ticking of a clock or of a metronome.

A *beat* is a metric unit formed by grouping two or three pulses. The physical means of grouping varies; it may take the form of accented and unaccented pulses, heavy and light pulses, active and passive pulses. In any case one part of the beat is perceived as a focal point or center, and the other as leading toward that focal point. Perhaps the relation of these two parts of the beat is most significantly expressed by the Greek words *arsis* and *thesis*, since they imply motion and repose, which are the essence of rhythm. As Aristoxenos explains, "When we lift our foot in order to walk that motion is *arsis*, and when we put it on the ground that act of posing is *thesis*." [4]

Two kinds of beats may be distinguished: *duple beats*, consisting of two pulses, and *triple beats*, consisting of three pulses. In duple beats the thesis and arsis are of equal length; in triple beats they are of unequal length, the first two pulses normally constituting the thesis and the third the arsis.

In music that is made up of not more than two note values the shorter

---

3. "We must imagine," he says, "two different natures, that of rhythm and that of rhythmizomenon, having the same relation to one another as a plan has to the object planned." Quoted in C. F. Abdy Williams, *The Aristoxenian Theory of Musical Rhythm*, Cambridge, 1911, p. 26.

4. Ἄρσιν ποίαν λέγομεν εἶναι; ὅταν μετέωρος ᾖ ὁ πούς ἡνίκα ἂν μέλλωμεν ἐμβαίνειν. Θέσιν δέ ποίαν; ὅταν κείμενος. Quoted in R. Westphal, *Die Fragmente und Lehrsätze der griechischen Rhythmiker*, 1861, p. 67, line 6.

duration will always represent the pulse, the longer the beat. In "metrical" music, which includes most of the occidental repertoire since the fourteenth century, beats as well as pulses are usually grouped regularly in series of twos or threes, forming *measures*. In the same way that one pulse of a beat is felt to outweigh the other in importance, one beat of the measure is felt to be more important; in other words it is more thetic than the other(s). Thus the beats of a measure stand in arsic and thetic relationship as do the pulses of a beat. In modern musical notation a measure is included between two barlines, which are so placed that each barline immediately precedes the thetic beat of the measure. It should be noted, however, that the space between two barlines was not always identical to a true measure. Regular measures may often be perceived in music that was written without barlines. Seventeenth-century composers most often used barlines to measure off units of time equivalent to the tactus. The tactus was a fixed duration of time assigned to a certain note value and used for the purpose of maintaining a steady tempo in conducting music. This time unit regulated the *durations* of the note values of which it was composed, but since it made no implications as to their *grouping* it did not necessarily correspond either to the beat or to the measure. Consequently, the assumption that the seventeenth-century barline is equivalent to the measure line of later notational practice will often lead to a distortion of the true meter of the music. One of the chief problems of interpretation of the music of this period is the discovery of the true measure. This point will be discussed at greater length in Chapter III, which deals with the relation of tactus to meter.

Because of the hierarchical nature of the meter of Western music, in which note values can be subdivided indefinitely, an ambiguity sometimes arises between its basic elements—pulse, beat, and measure. Each duration in the metric hierarchy may be construed as a subdivision of the next longer duration, and vice versa. If the note values representing pulses are consistently subdivided or if the tempo is slowed down the pulses may be perceived as beats and their subdivisions as pulses. At the other end of the scale, if the tempo is accelerated what were beats may be felt as pulses of beats on the next higher level. This phenomenon is perhaps most obvious in the case of so-called "compound time" such as $\frac{6}{8}$, which is normally felt as two triple beats per measure, but if there are many sixteenth notes, or if the tempo is sufficiently slow, it may turn out to represent six duple beats per measure. Actually not only the so-called "compound meters" but *all* meters are compound in this sense, and two levels are often perceptible at the same time. In waltzes written in $\frac{3}{4}$ time, for instance, the measures invariably proceed in groups of twos or fours and each measure is actually felt as a beat, so that the meter would be more accurately described as *duple* groups of *triple* beats. Moreover, if the quarter note pulses of these beats are consistently subdivided one can quite easily perceive two levels of meter simultaneously, and by shifting the focus of one's attention can bring one or another of the metric levels to the foreground. It appears, then, that the ambiguity of the terms "beat," "pulse," and "measure" is not merely semantic but is inherent in the nature of these constituents of the metric hierarchy. In order to avoid confusion, in our discussions of meter, it therefore behooves us to specify in each case to which level the "beat" of which we are speaking belongs.

The hierarchical organization of pulses, beats, and measures is the metric scheme upon which the activity of rhythm is to be exerted. The act of "rhythming" is essentially that of transforming the temporal durations provided by meter into patterns of motion and repose. Pulses, beats, and measures might go on forever in a regular succession of arses and theses did not the occurrence of particularly thetic beats mark momentary points of repose in the flow of the music. These stopping-places, which Aristoxenos calls "resting places for the mind," divide the music into rhythmic units of varying degrees of completeness analogous to the varying degrees of pause in discourse implied by punctuation marks such as the comma, semi-colon, colon, and period. Two or more of the smaller units are included in each larger unit, and the articulations become progressively more conclusive as the units become larger. The observance of the degree of motion and repose proper to each of these divisions is the most important factor in the rhythmic performance of music. If the articulations are obliterated the performance will be mechanical and dull; if they are overemphasized or improperly placed it will become disjointed or chaotic. Yet musical notation has no effective means of indicating these divisions, nor does our current terminology include adequate names for them. A hierarchy of terms such as *motive*, *phrase member*, *phrase*, *period*, *section* would be useful if employed with any degree of consistency, which is not usually the case.

A *rhythmic pattern* may coincide in length with any one of these divisions. It must have a definite beginning and end, which meter, as such, does not. It also frequently contains a *rhythmic climax*, which may be defined as a beat that marks a point of arrival in relation to the preceding beats yet is not the final thetic beat of the pattern. A feminine cadence, for example, invariably has a rhythmic climax that is comparable to the penultimate syllable of a paroxytone word. A rhythmic pattern does not necessarily coincide with a measure or with any given number of measures. Indeed, rhythmic patterns and measures almost inevitably overlap since the *first* beat of a measure is thetic, while the *last* beat of the rhythmic pattern is thetic. In other words, rhythmic patterns usually straddle barlines.

An adequate description of a rhythmic pattern should take account of all the factors mentioned and defined above. It should therefore include information concerning the following points: (1) the level of meter on which the principal action takes place and the relation of the beats on this level to those on other levels; (2) the length of the pattern in numbers of beats; (3) the position of relatively thetic beats within the pattern, which establish the constitution of the measures and the appropriate placing of barlines in modern notation; (4) the point of rhythmic climax.

Notations and Transcriptions

All musical notation is symbolic. In the last analysis its notes and signs function chiefly as reminders to the musician of tonal patterns and rhythms with which he is already familiar. The musicians of the Renaissance, for instance, were almost exclusively concerned with absolute and relative durations of notes of various time values. Now while certain configurations of note values may *suggest* certain rhythmic and metric groupings, the time values in themselves do not constitute rhythm or meter. The fact that the notation of the seventeenth century, as well as that of the Renaissance, often lacks explicit indications of metric and rhythmic groupings does not mean that such groupings did not occur in actual performance. It means only that once the problems of duration—often exceedingly complex—were solved, the grouping of pulses and beats into patterns could be left to the musical intelligence of the performers because, however numerous and complicated they may have been, these were familiar patterns that formed part of the musical experience of the average musician.

To confront the twentieth-century performer with a bare series of notes in a style with which he is not familiar, and to expect him to divine the proper metric and rhythmic groupings is a very different matter. The chief problem of the transcriber of music of past periods lies in the fact that he is dealing with two systems that must be reconciled: the notation that sufficed for the composers and performers of the time, and modern notation. Many transcribers have evaded this problem by evolving a third, or compromise system which might be called "transcribers' " notation and which corresponds to neither. This consists in translating the note values into their modern equivalents, then laying them out between mechanically placed barlines —which inevitably have metrical connotations to trained musicians—then finally instructing the executants to disregard these barlines and "let the music speak for itself." Unfortunately notation is not music, and cannot speak at all except through the musical experience of whoever reads it.

If there is one point in which modern notation shows a superiority over that of the sixteenth and seventeenth centuries it is its capacity to indicate more precisely (though still not altogether precisely) the desired metrical groupings and changes of measure. Yet this capacity is rarely if ever exploited by transcribers, presumably through a fear of reading something into the score that was not intended by the composer. The effect of such discretion is, of course, merely to shift the responsibility to the performer or conductor or to the editor who concocts a "practical edition." For when the composer's intentions are not explicit in his notation *someone* must interpret them if they are to come out as music at all. The question is, who is best qualified to do the interpretation, the transcriber, who works from original sources and has presumably studied the music he is transcribing and many other works similar to it, or the performer or editor, who may or may not be familiar with the style of the period, and who has before him only what is provided by the transcriber? It seems more than likely that the blame for a great many dull, unmusical performances of early music can be laid at the door of transcribers who have shirked their responsibility.

This brings up the question of just how much the transcriber should alter and add to a seventeenth-century score. If a modern edition is to be of any use as a guide to performance it must include numerous features of execution that are not explicit in the original. The realization of the *basso continuo*, for example, has long been accepted as a necessary addition; without it most keyboard players would be quite unable to provide a satisfactory harmonic background. Many modern editions also offer indications for bowing, phrasing, and articulation, as well as suggestions regarding tempo and dynamics, all of which are lacking in most seventeenth-century scores. The addition of appropriate ornamentation to replace that which was originally improvised is less generally recognized as essential; it is found only to a very limited extent in a few publications edited by musicologists. Virtually no editors of modern editions of works by Monteverdi, Gabrieli, Frescobaldi, and their contemporaries have taken the trouble to find the modern equivalents of the metric and rhythmic aspects of the original notation.

All these factors—all aspects of the music, indeed, except the relative pitches of the notes and their relative duration—are matters of interpretation. No interpretation can be completely authoritative. The transcriber's duty, it seems to me, is to provide as complete an interpretation as possible, including suggestions for all phases of execution, but at the same time to leave the way open for alternative interpretations. This can only be done by presenting the music in such a way that there is a clear distinction between what is interpretation and what is not. The transcriber's additions, whether notes or markings, should be differentiated typographically from those set down by the composer; if note values, time signatures, or barrings are altered their original form should be indicated. Then if a performer or a scholar desires to make a different interpretation he can, if he wishes, reconstruct the original score and start from scratch.

One further suggestion may be offered to transcribers and editors of early music. Would it not be a help to the performer if the visual aspect of the music as it appears on the printed page had some relation to the structure of the music as it is meant to sound? A piece of music, like a poem, is heard as a series of rhythmic units, with articulations marking the beginnings and endings of phrases, periods, and sections. These musical units are of the same nature as the lines and stanzas of a poem. If poems were printed in such a way that the lines and stanzas were run together filling the entire width of the page the reader would have some difficulty detecting their rhythmic structure. Yet this is the accepted procedure in music printing. Neither publishers, editors, nor even composers make any effort to utilize the physical appearance of the music on the page as a means of communication.

In the Anthology that accompanies this volume an attempt has been made to clarify the rhythmic structure of the music through its placement on the page. The lengths of the individual lines are governed not by the width of the page but by the articulations of the music, the texts, and the dance patterns. Performers who are accustomed to reading by bars may find it disconcerting that lines sometimes end in the middle of a measure—a natural consequence of the fact that rhythmic patterns normally straddle barlines. In my opinion the gain in rhythmic clarity outweighs this slight obstruction to the mechanics of sight reading. Of this the reader may judge for himself. The procedure is admittedly experimental, but may be found to have definite advantages, especially as a means of interpreting music that is written in an unfamiliar idiom.

TWO

MUSICAL NOTATION IN ITALY IN THE SEVENTEENTH CENTURY

Theoretical Sources

THE SEVENTEENTH CENTURY WAS A PERIOD OF TRANSITION AND EXPERIMENTATION in musical notation; one is not surprised to find in the musical sources many deviations from any set of theoretical rules. Nevertheless, certain norms can be established from the following works, which contain information pertinent to the state of notation and its relation to performance during the early part of the century:

Antonio Brunelli—*Regole utilissime per li scolari*, Florence, 1606
Gio. Batt. Olifante—*Trattato Brevissimo intorno alle Proportioni cantabili.* Printed as an appendix to Rocco Rodio's *Regole di musica*, Naples, 1608 (dated 1611)
Agostino Pisa—*Battuta della musica dichiarata*, Rome, 1611
S. Picerli—*Specchio di Musica*, Vol. 1, Naples, 1630
Gio. Filippo Cavalliere—*Il scolaro Principiante di Musica*, Naples, 1634
Horatio Scaletta—*Scala di Musica coretta & aggiuntovi alcune cose bisognevole da . . . M.A. Grancino*, Milan, 1657

Of particular value is Brunelli's *Regole*, because it was written specifically for the guidance of performers and because it is the work of a practicing musician and teacher who was only secondarily a theorist. Antonio Brunelli, *maestro di capella* to the Grand Duke of Tuscany, composed music for the carnevali at Pisa and for the order of Cavalieri di S. Stefano there. He was for some time organist at San Miniato in Florence and had a wide reputation as a teacher of composition and singing. His *Varii esercitii*, published in 1614, are exercises for singers which he composed in connection with his duties as singing teacher in the household of Don Antonio Medici and dedicated to his pupil, Signora Artemisia Torri. Each of his three books of *Scherzi, Canzoni, Arie e Madrigale* (1612, 1614, 1616), as well as his *Fioretti Spirituali* of 1626, contains a preface giving explicit directions for the performance of his works. Brunelli states, in the Introduction to his *Regole*, that he has studied music with many celebrated teachers, notably in Rome, and that in this book he has set down what he has learned from them as well as the results of his own practical experience. In spite of the early date of its publication the *Regole* can probably be accepted as applicable to the works of the composers in Brunelli's own immediate circle, which include most of those listed in Chapter I.[1] The following discussion of notational practices at the beginning of the seventeenth century is based primarily upon this book, supplemented when necessary by information drawn from the other works mentioned above.

The notes in use at this time were:

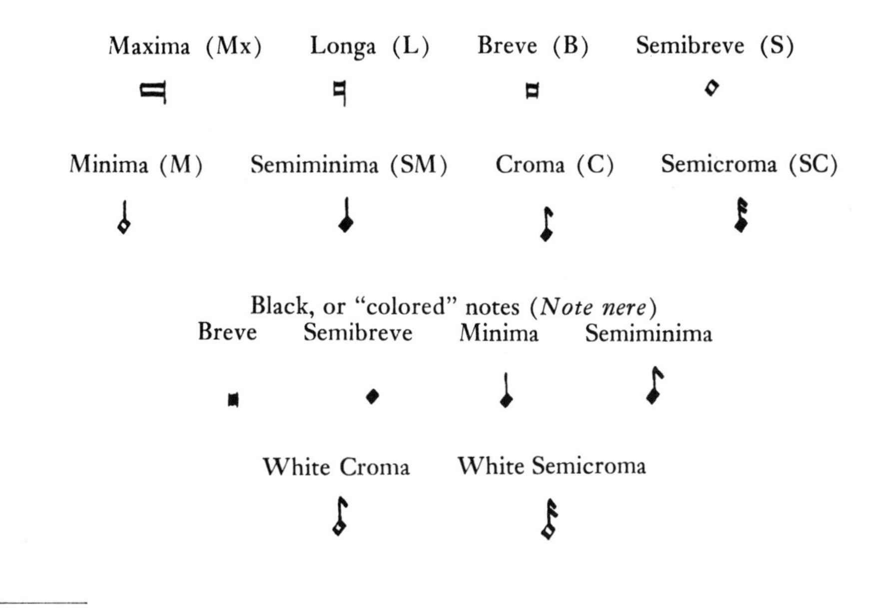

1. Cf. pp. 14–15 supra.

The relative values of these notes are variable to some extent in accordance with principles derived from the mensural notation of the sixteenth and previous centuries; these must be briefly summarized here in order to clarify the terminology used by Brunelli and his contemporaries.[2] Whereas in modern notation an undotted note always equals two notes of the next smaller value, in mensural notation it may equal either two or three, depending upon the mensural sign placed at the beginning of the piece. The terms *modus*, *tempus*, and *prolatio* were used to refer to the relationships L:B, B:S, and S:M respectively. Ternary relationships were termed *perfect*, binary relationships *imperfect*. Under certain conditions a perfect note could be rendered imperfect, that is, deprived of one third of its value, by a process known as *imperfection*. In perfect mensurations a short note could be doubled in value in order to fill out the *perfection* (triple duration) required by the value of the next higher species: this process was known as *alteration*. Black, or "colored" notes were always imperfect, even in perfect mensurations.

Tempus perfectum, in which B = three S, was indicated by a whole circle, O; *tempus imperfectum*, in which B = two S, was indicated by a semicircle open at the right, C.

Further variations in the durations of note values were brought about by the use of proportions, that is by the diminution or augmentation of their values in certain arithmetical ratios. *Proportio dupla*, simple diminution in the ratio 2:1, was indicated by a stroke through the circle of *tempus perfectum*, ⦶ or through the semicircle of *tempus imperfectum*, ₵. The signs for the other proportions took the form of fractions, $\frac{3}{1}$, $\frac{3}{2}$, etc., specifying the arithmetical ratio desired. *Prolatio perfecta*, in which S = three M, could occur in combination with *tempus perfectum* or *tempus imperfectum*. It was indicated by a dot placed in the center of the circle, ⊙, or semicircle, ☉. In the absence of the dot, *prolatio imperfecta* was to be assumed and the S, unless augmented by a dot, was equal to two M.

All the mensural signs described above continue to be found in the music of the early seventeenth century, and remain in force with little change in meaning. The terminology used by the theorists, however, is somewhat different and reflects a modification in the practical application of the signs to performance. In the first place, the fact that the signs for *proportio dupla* are not considered separately but are treated as qualifications of the *tempus* suggests that the word *tempo*, rather than being restricted to the relationship of

2. For a more detailed explanation of the principles of mensural notation cf. W. Apel, *The Notation of Polyphonic Music*, Cambridge, Mass., 1944, Part II, pp. 89–188.

B to S is beginning to have implications that correspond to its modern significance of *rate of speed.* Brunelli, for instance, designates as *tempo maggiore imperfetto* (major imperfect tempus) the sign which earlier theorists called simply *tempus imperfectum,* while the sign ₵ becomes *tempo minore imperfetto* (minor imperfect tempus). Further concern for the rate of speed in performance is seen in Brunelli's treatment of the proportions. *Proportio tripla,* $\frac{3}{1}$, and *sesquialtera,* $\frac{3}{2}$, had, of course, long been used in conjunction with various mensuration signs. Now, however, Brunelli carefully distinguishes between major and minor proportions and between major and minor sesquialtera according to *which* note value corresponds to the tactus under each combination of signs.

All the theorists of the early seventeenth century, indeed, take special pains to indicate how many notes of each time value are to be performed to the duration of a tactus (*battuta*)—a regular unit of time measured by a downward and upward motion of the hand (*positio* and *levatio, battere* and *levare,* or, as Brunelli graphically puts it, *in terra* and *in aria*). The relationship of note values to a standard temporal unit was, of course, implicit in the earlier mensural system, but heretofore theorists had not taken the trouble to codify it for each individual combination of signs. Brunelli frequently specifies which notes are to be performed on the downward stroke of the hand and which on the upstroke. The technique of adjusting the notes to the motions of the hand must have been very highly developed at this time, for Agostino Pisa devotes his entire treatise, *Battuta della musica dichiarata,* to this subject. In it he discusses at length such subtle and specialized problems as the following: (1)What motion does the hand make before raising it to begin the stroke? (2)At what point does the tactus actually begin—while the hand is still raised or at the instant it reaches the bottom of the stroke? (3)How many notes are to be performed during the time that the hand is moving in the air? (This is illustrated by means of oblique lines on the page, along which are placed notes of various values.) (4)Does the hand stop moving at the bottom of the stroke, and if so for how long? (In the case of triple note values the first third is performed while the hand is moving down, the second while the hand is at rest and the third during the upstroke. (5)Is the final note of every piece to be cut off when the hand reaches the top of its last stroke?

The modifications undergone by the mensural system as well as the differences between seventeenth-century notation and that of the present time can probably best be elucidated through quotations from the explicit directions given in Brunelli's *Regole.*

The Four Tempi

1. *Tempo maggiore imperfetto*, C, means that under this sign the Mx lasts eight tactus, the L four, the B two, the S one, the M one half, the SM one fourth, the C one eighth, the SC one sixteenth of a tactus. Or, for greater clarity we may say the M go two to a tactus, SM four, C eight, and SC sixteen.[3]

2. *Tempo minore imperfetto*, ¢, can be regulated [conducted] in two ways. The first is that it can be sung like the *maggiore imperfetto* [two M to a tactus, but presumably with a faster tactus]. The second is that it should be sung with all the notes and rests at half value [two S per tactus] and this is its proper meaning. If many masters teach the singing of this *tempo* in the same way as the *maggiore imperfetto* they do so in order to lessen the difficulty for their students, and perhaps some do it through ignorance. And that this is true can be seen in many printed compositions in which the rules of this *tempo* have not been observed. For the experts know very well that the *tempo minore*, whether perfect or imperfect, should always be composed with an uneven number of notes so that it can be sung at half value. For example, if it is composed of five S to be sung alternately on downstroke and upstroke the fifth will come on the downstroke and will finish off the tactus. Whereas if there were four, alternating on downstroke and upstroke, the fourth would end in the air; yet this *tempo* should be sung at half value. It is true enough that it *can* be sung as above, taking one S per tactus, but this is done only to reduce the difficulty of singing it, not because it is correct.[4]

Although Brunelli does not explain precisely what the difficulty is in singing the *tempo minore* at half value, it would seem to be due to the fact that

---

3. Brunelli, *Regole*, p. 16. "Il Tempo Maggiore imperfetto denota che sotto lui la Massima vale otto battute, la Longa quattro, la Breve due; la Semibreve una, la Minima mezza, la Semiminima un quarto, la Croma un'ottavo, & la Semicroma la sestadecima parte d'una battuta. O vero per più chiarezza diciamo, che delle Minime ne vanno due per battuta, delle Simiminime quattro: delle Crome otto, & delle Semicrome seidici."

4. *Ibid.*, p. 17. "Il Tempo Minore imperfetto si può regolare in due modi, il primo è che si può cantare come Maggiore imperfetto, il secondo è che si devono cantare tutte le sue Note per metà, si come ancora le Pause si conteranno per metà, & questo è il suo proprio, e se alcuni Maestri l'insegnano à cantare come Maggiore imperfetto lo fanno per levare la difficultà allo scolare, e forse alcuni lo fanno per ignoranza. E che sia la verità si vede in molte Compositioni d'alcuni che hanno stampato non essere osservata la Regola di detti Tempi. Perchè sanno bene i periti che il Tempo Minore tanto imperfetto quanto perfetto si deve comporre sempre di numero impari acciò si possi cantare per metà, come per essempio se fate cinque Semibrevi, mettendone una in terra, & una in aria la quinta verrà in terra, e terminerà la Battuta & se fossero quattro, mettendone una in terra, & una in aria la quarta nota finirebbe in aria, però detto Tempo si deve cantare per metà. E ben vero che si può cantare come sopra mandando una Semibreve a battuta: ma questo si fa per levare la difficultà al cantare, non già che sia suo proprio."

too many notes would have to be adjusted to each motion of the hand because of the excessive slowness of the tactus. This would imply that the *tempo minore* when sung like the *maggiore* (S = tactus) would employ a tactus that moves faster, but not necessarily twice as fast as that of the *maggiore*.

> 3. *Tempo maggiore perfetto*, O, is sung in the same way as *tempo maggiore imperfetto* [S = tactus] apart from this difference: that some rests are perfect and some notes can be sometimes perfect and sometimes altered.[5]

The rules for perfection and alteration that follow here are similar to those of the sixteenth century except that Brunelli follows his usual procedure of specifying the actual duration of the notes in terms of tactus. They may be summarized as follows: (a) A B followed by another B, by a L or by two or three S is perfect and lasts three tactus. (b) A B followed or preceded by a single S or more than three S is imperfect and lasts only two tactus. (c) When two S occur between two B the second S is altered (doubled in value) and lasts two tactus. (d) B rests, like B, are perfect and can cause perfection under conditions (a) and (b) but cannot be imperfected. (e) S rests, like S, are imperfect and can cause imperfection under rule (c), but cannot be altered. (f) The dot of division is used to annul rules (a) and (b) by marking the end of a perfection. Brunelli gives the following examples illustrating perfection, imperfection, alteration, and the dot of division. The figures indicate the number of tactus.[6]

Perfection Imperfection Alteration Dot of Division

As a matter of fact the two *tempi perfetti*, O and Φ, occur very rarely in the music of this period except when these signs are followed by numbers denoting proportions. An understanding of the rules of perfection and alteration is necessary, however, in order to read the music written under the signs O $\frac{3}{2}$, and Φ $\frac{3}{2}$, which are fairly common.

> 4. *Tempo minore perfetto*, O, should be sung in the same way as the *minore imperfetto*, that is, by half values [B = tactus], and this is its proper

5. *Ibid.*, p. 17. "Il Tempo Maggiore perfetto va cantato nel medesimo modo, che il Maggiore imperfetto, postposta la differenzia, che è in alcune Pause, & alcune Note che alle volte sono perfette, & altre volte alterate."
6. *Ibid.*, p. 20.

> nature. It can also be sung in the ordinary manner like the *tempo maggiore imperfetto* except for its perfections and alterations, which are these: the rests that touch two lines of the staff and those that touch three lines and also the following notes: Mx, L, B, and S, in short all the perfections and alterations of notes as well as rests and all the other "accidentals" [e.g. the dot of division] that are found in this tempo are regulated as has been explained above in connection with the *tempo maggiore perfetto*. . . . Notice, however, that if it is sung at half value *all* the notes will have half value, as well as the rests.[7]

Brunelli's last statement clearly indicates the following relationships for the *tempo minore perfetto:*

perfect B = 1½ tactus
imperfect B = 1 tactus
altered S = 1 tactus
S = ½ tactus
M = ¼ tactus

It should be noted that Brunelli includes the Mx and the L among the notes that can be perfect and cause perfection in *tempo perfetto*. This implies that perfect *modus* and perfect *maximodus* are still at least theoretically possible, though no examples are given of either.

Brunelli makes no mention of barlines, nor do any of the other theorists of the time. Barlines do occur, however, in practically all the manuscripts and prints of the period, including Brunelli's own publications, whenever the music consists of two parts only (solo and *basso continuo*). On rare occasions compositions with as many as six or seven parts are scored and therefore barred, as in Lorenzo Allegri's *Primo Libro di Musiche*, 1618, where the composer explains in a note that "I wished to present the Sinfonie in score [*spartite*] for the greater convenience of the perfect instruments such as the lute, the organ, and particularly the double harp." [8] Barlines are customarily placed at intervals corresponding to the duration of a tactus as in Brunelli's aria:

---

7. *Ibid.*, p. 21. "Il Tempo Minore perfetto si doverebbe cantare nel medesimo modo del Minore imperfetto cioe per metà, e questo è il suo proprio, & anco si può cantare ordinariamente come il Tempo Maggiore imperfetto postposto le perfezioni, & alterazioni che vi sono quale sono queste. Le battute che toccano due righe, e quelle che ne toccano tre, & ancora le Note seguenti: Massima, Longa, Breve, & Semibreve, & per maggior brevità tutte le perfezioni, & alterazioni, tanto nelle Note, quanto nelle Pause & tutti gl'altri accidenti, che si trovano in detto Tempo tutti si regolano come nel Tempo Maggiore perfetto, s'è già detto di sopra, perchè s'osserva la medesima regola . . . ma se si canta per metà tutte le Note varranno la metà manco tanto le perfette, quanto l'imperfette, come anco le Pause."

8. Allegri, L. *Il Primo Libro*, p. 1. "Ho voluto situare le Sinfonie spartite per commodità dell'Istrumenti perfetti come Liuto, Organo, e in particolare dell'Arpa doppia."

EX. 1

Sometimes, however, the bar embraces two tactus, as in the following song, also by Brunelli:

EX. 2

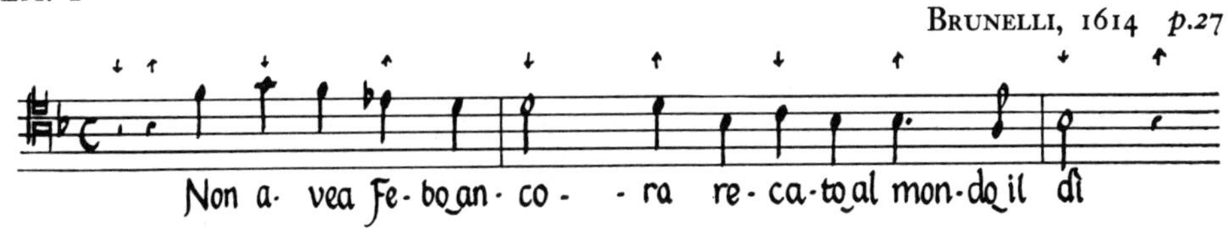

An anonymous composition on p. 60 of the Barbera MS, which turns out to be the song that opens Act II of Monteverdi's *Orfeo*, is written in *tempo minore imperfetto*. Barlines are at first placed according to tactus, but when the music does not come out even the scribe is forced to include bars of half a tactus:

EX. 3

This is an example of the case referred to by Brunelli in which the rules of the *tempo* have not been observed, with the result that the melody "ends in the air." It should, of course, have been written in *tempo maggiore imperfetto*, C, with S = tactus, and does, in fact, appear under this sign on another page of the same manuscript (p. 300), as well as in the 1609 edition of Monteverdi's opera.

A similar case by Marco da Gagliano is barred by half tactus, and also ends wrongly "in the air":

EX. 4

M. GAGLIANO *p.6*

Al- ma mia do- vè ten va- - i Al- ma mia chi fug- gi tu?

It is quite obvious here that Gagliano intended the piece to be performed with one tactus per bar—a procedure which, as we have seen, was optional even under Brunelli's strict rules—and that the composer used the sign ₵ for another reason, namely to suggest a faster moving tactus than would have been implied by the unbarred C. Thus we can see that the tendency to dissociate the sign ₵ from *alla breve* performance (B = tactus) and to use it as an indication of a faster tempo than C was strong even at this time, though this usage was not officially accepted by theorists until the second half of the century.

Numbers and Proportions

In a chapter entitled *De numeri* Brunelli states a rule that applies not only to the proportions that may occur in the course of a piece but also to the signatures that indicate the various kinds of *tripla* (i.e. *proportione maggiore* and *minore*, *sesquialtera maggiore* and *minore*, and *emiolia maggiore* and *minore*) although he later devotes an entire chapter to each of these:

> Sometimes in singing one comes across certain numbers that cause no little embarrassment to singers who do not know what they mean. However, in order to understand them easily one must first notice what *tempo* was indicated at the beginning of the piece. For instance, if *tempo maggiore imperfetto* were indicated by means of the sign C and later there should follow some sort of number, notice that there will always be *two* such numbers, one above the other. The lower number will refer to the *tempo* that has been sung so far and the upper number to the *tempo* that should be sung from now on. That is, the lower number will state that where at first there were two S or two M to the tactus, depending on which of these numbers will previously have been indicated, there will be from now on as many of this kind of note per tactus as is specified by the upper number. If, for example, the two numbers $\frac{2}{1}$ should occur, the 1 below indicates that previously there was one note per tactus, and the 2 states that there should now be two per tactus. Therefore you must know which kind of note originally went one to a tactus, which kind went two to a tactus and so forth. . . . If the number $\frac{1}{2}$ should appear it means that where previously two notes went to a tactus there will now be only one of that kind of note . . . it is also especially necessary to notice that when pieces have the signs for *tempi minori*, whether perfect or imperfect, they should be sung at half value, because the lower number will always refer to the notes as if they were sung at half value. But the singer is not actually obliged to sing them at half value. If, however, these signs should not be mixed with signs for *tempo maggiore* it is true that they should be sung at half value, but for more facility they are sung in the ordinary way.[9]

9. Brunelli, *op. cit.*, p. 22. "Alle volte cantando si trovano varii numeri, i quali à molti

By far the most common use of numbers was to indicate, in combination with *tempo* signs, the various kinds of *tripla*, that is, groups of three notes to be performed in the time which, according to the *tempo*, is alloted to one or to two. Brunelli divides *tripla* into three categories: (1) *proportioni*, in which the original tempo is perfect, (2) *sesquialtera*, in which the original *tempo* is imperfect, and (3) *emiolia*, in which triple groups are written in black notes. One feature that all three *tripla* have in common is the use, in performance, of *tactus inaequalis*, the first two notes of each triple group being performed on the downstroke of the tactus and the third on the upstroke.

1. *Proportione maggiore* can be designated in two ways: O $\frac{3}{1}$ or ⦶ $\frac{3}{2}$. If the rule of numbers is applied it will be seen that the 1 of the first sign refers to the S (one per tactus under O), and that the 2 of the second sign likewise refers to the S (two per tactus under ⦶) so that each sign demands three S per tactus. Being written in *tempo perfetto*, the *proportione maggiore* requires the perfection of the B and the alteration of the S according to the rules given above. Exceptions to the rule must be indicated by the use of black notes, which are always imperfect and prevent both perfection and alteration; cf. Example 5a.

2. *Sesquialtera maggiore* is indicated by ¢ $\frac{3}{2}$ or C $\frac{3}{1}$. (See Ex. 5b.) Applying the rule of numbers we find that it also requires three S per tactus, but since it is written in *tempo imperfetto* no perfections or alterations are involved. Brunelli remarks, however, that "this rule is little observed by some authors who want a B before another B to be perfect and who give to others perfection and alteration. . . . I do not know what reasoning they can follow. How can a B before another B or before a rest that causes perfection in *proportione maggiore* be perfect in *sesquialtera maggiore*, which is written under the sign of *tempo minore imperfetto*? How can they also wish to introduce alteration in *sesquialtera* . . . ? Besides, if there were no difference

cantori non poca difficultà apportano per non sapere quello voglino significare. Però bisogna avvertire che Tempo è segnato nel principio della cantilena per volergli intendere facilmente, come per esempio se fosse segnato in Tempo Maggiore imperfetto come qui C & poi seguitasse qualsivoglia numero bisogna avvertire che sempre detti numeri saranno due, cioè uno sopra, & l'altro sotto; quello di sotto denoterà il Tempo s'è cantato, & quel di sopra quel che si deve cantare, cioè quello di sotto dirà che dove prima mandavi due semibrevi, o due Minime à battuta secondo che sarà segnato il numero già detto, se ne metterà poi tante à battuta quante dimostrerà il numero di sopra. Come per esempio se si troverassero segnati due numeri cosi $\frac{2}{1}$ quello 1 di sotto accenna che prima n'andava una à battuta, & il 2 dice che se ne mandino due per battuta. Avvertendo di sapere quale è quella Nota che valeva una battuta, quale due, & cosi dell'altre. . . . si trovasse il numero segnato cosi $\frac{1}{2}$ accenna che dove prima n'andavano due à battuta essendovi detti numeri n'andrà una solamente . . . Devesi poi grandemente avvertire che quando saranno segnate le Cantilene con i Tempi Minori tanto col Minore perfetto, quanto col Minore imperfetto, si devono cantare per metà perche i numeri di sotto sempre accenneranno le Note come se si cantassero per metà, ma non forzeranno già il cantore che le canti per metà: se però non vi fossero mescolati i Tempi Maggiori, è ben vero che si dovrebbono cantare per metà, ma per facilità si cantanò all'ordinario."

between *proportione maggiore* and *sesquialtera maggiore* it would not be necessary to use *sesquialtera* in some cases and *proportione* in others." [10] At any rate, this common misconception must be the reason why black notes are frequently employed in *sesquialtera* in order to avoid any ambiguity that might arise.

3. "*Emiolia maggiore* is that which is written in black notes and in which three S go to a tactus, that is two *in terra* and the third *in aria;* it is sung in the same way as *sesquialtera maggiore* and the rests also have the same values." [11] (See Ex. 5c.)

The following Table shows the same series of notes and their relation to the tactus under each of the foregoing triple signatures:

TABLE I

	Signature	Tactus
Tempo maggiore perfetto	O	1 2 3 4 5 6 7 8 9 10 11 12 13 14 15
Tempo minore perfetto	Φ	1 2 3 4 5 6 7 8
Proportione maggiore	Φ 3/2	1 2 3 4 5
Sesquialtera maggiore	¢ 3/2	1 2 3 4
	¢ 3/2	1 2 3 4
Emiolia maggiore	¢	1 2 3 4

10. *Ibid.*, p. 26. ". . . benche questa regola sia poco osservata da alcuni Autori, che vogliono che una Breve quando è appresso all'altra sia perfetta; & ancora li danno altre perfezioni, & alterazioni. Io non sò con che ragione lo faccino; perchè come potrà essere che la Breve posta avanti alla sua simile, o vero alle Pause, che danno perfezione nella Proportione Maggiore, nella Sesq. Magg. segnata in Tempo Minore imperfetto sia perfetta? come vogliono ancora, che segua l'alterazione nella Semibreve? . . . In oltre se non fosse differenza tra la Proportione Maggiore, & la Sesquialtera Maggiore non occorrerebbe tal volta fare la Sesquialtera & tal'hora la Proportione."

11. *Ibid.*, p. 28. "L'Emiolia Maggiore è quella, che è fatta di Note nere, nella quale vanne tre Semibrevi à Battuta, cioè due in terra, & la terza in aria, & si canta nel medesimo modo, che la Sesquialtera Maggiore, e anco le Pause, hanno le medesima valsuta . . ."

It will be observed that the identical series of notes occupies 15, 7½, 5, and 4 tactus according to their signature. Assuming the tactus to retain approximately the same duration, four different tempos (in the modern sense) are thus indicated. The black notes in the second version of *sequialtera maggiore* are not really necessary but, as remarked above, they are very often used to avoid possible confusion with *proportione maggiore.* The *sesquialtera maggiore* and the *emiolia maggiore* are seen to be identical in effect. The all-black notation of the *emiolia* was presumably used to avoid the frequent shifts from white to black notes and vice versa.

The following examples are the first phrases of three gagliardas by Lorenzo Allegri. The black notes in Example 5a are used to prevent the perfection of the B and the alteration of the second S that would be required by the signature.

EX. 5

4. "*Proportione minore* is indicated thus O $\frac{3}{2}$ which shows that there are three M to a tactus, that is, two on the downstroke and one on the upstroke. The rests ordinarily have the same value as though there were no proportion. . . . In this proportion arise the perfection of the S and the alteration of the M, which follow the same rules as the perfection and alteration in *tempo perfetto maggiore.* Black S and M are counted as though they were imperfect white S and M; these notes are used to prevent perfection and alteration." [12]

12. *Ibid.*, p. 27. "La Proportione Minore si segna sotto questo Tempo come qui O $\frac{3}{2}$ qual segno dimostra, che vanno tre Minime à Battuta, cioè due in terra & una in aria, e le pause vagliono ordinariamente come se non fosse proportione . . . In questa Proportione nasce la perfezione alla Semibreve, & l'alterazione nella Minima . . . La Semibreve, & Minima nera varranno come se fossero bianche imperfette, le quali Note son fatte per levare l'alterazione, & perfezione."

5. "*Sesquialtera minore* is indicated thus C$\frac{3}{2}$, and is sung in the same manner as *proportione minore* except for the perfections that are used in that *proportione*, because in this *sesquialtera* no perfections of any sort arise, since it has the sign of *tempo imperfetto*, in which perfections cannot occur." [13]

EX. 6

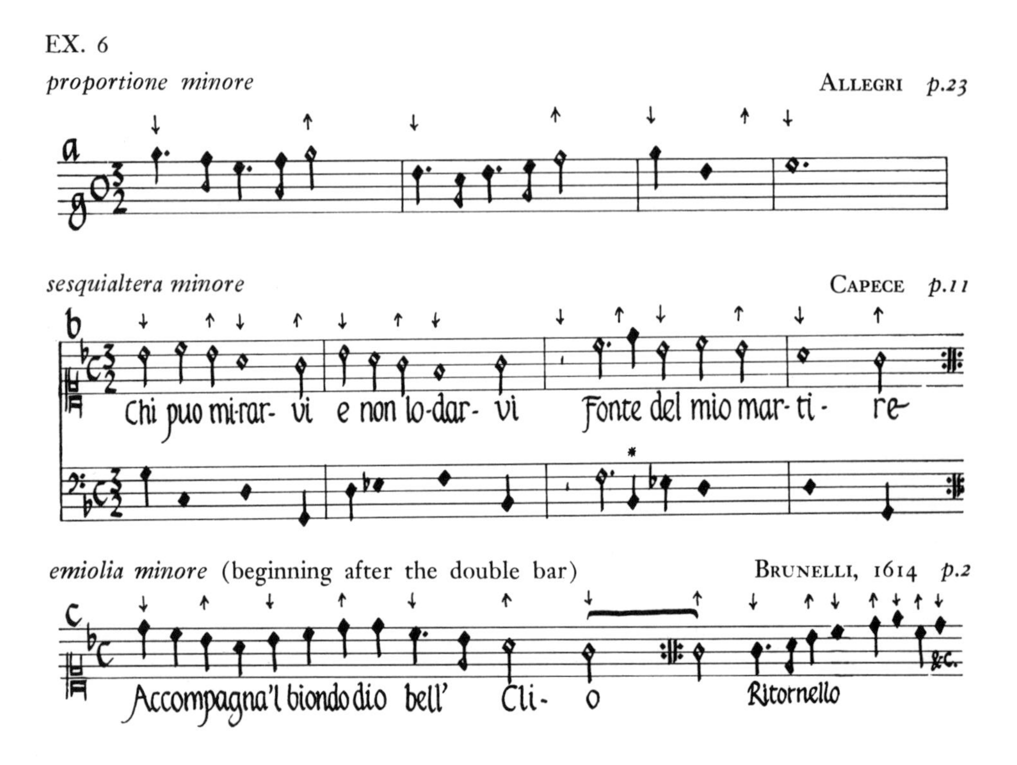

6. "*Emiolia minore* is indicated by the sign of *tempo maggiore imperfetto* C and is written in black notes. In it there are three black M to a tactus. That is, two on the downstroke and one on the upstroke. It is sung in the same way as *proportione minore* . . ." [14] except for the perfections. In other words it is identical in effect with *sesquialtera minore*. They can therefore be used together, or even mixed, as in Example 6b by Capece, in which the bass is almost entirely in black notation. Notice that the B♭ in the bass marked with an asterisk is a SM, whereas the next note, though physically

13. *Ibid.*, p. 28. "La Sesquialtera Minore si segna con questo Tempo C$\frac{3}{2}$ e và cantata nel medesimo modo che la Proportione minore eccettuate le Perfetioni, che fa detta Proportione, perche in questa Sesquialtera non ci nasce Perfetioni di sorte alcuna, per essere segnata in Tempo imperfetto il quale non può dare Perfetione."

14. *Ibid.*, p. 29. "L'Emiolia minore si segna nel Tempo Maggiore imperfetto, & è di Note nere, & in essa vanno tre Minime nere à Battuta, cioè due in terra, & uno in aria; & si canta nel medesimo modo, che la Proportione minore & le Pause hanno la medesima valsuta."

identical with it, is a black M and has twice its value.

In Example 6a, from a gagliarda by Allegri, the S in the third bar is black to ensure its imperfection, and the black M in the same bar has the same value as the white M which precedes it. Example 6c, by Brunelli, shows the relation between *tempo maggiore imperfetto* and *emiolia minore*. The change takes place after the white minim following the double bar; the next note, a dotted black minim, begins the *emiolia*, and the *tactus inaequalis*, starting at this point, would presumably retain the same duration as the even tactus that precedes it.

7. "*Meliola*, which can be used under any *tempo* whatever, gives three black M to the tactus, two on the downstroke and one on the upstroke. It is customary to use it as in the following example, and every time no further 3 appears the *meliola* stops. One can come out of it either into black or into white notes." [15]

3 ♩. ♪ ♩ 3 ◆ ♩ 3 ♩. ♪ ♩ ◇

8. The proportion designated by the sign $C\frac{6}{4}$ is not described by Brunelli in his *Regole*. Nevertheless, it occurs frequently in his later musical publications and those of his contemporaries. Moreover, his rule of numbers clearly applies to this proportion; the fraction indicates that in place of the usual four SM per tactus under the sign C six are to be sung. The fact that no 3 occurs in the signature implies that an even rather than an uneven tactus should be used. This interpretation is corroborated by Horatio Scaletta, who writes: "And in these modern times there is also the *sesquiquarta*, $\frac{6}{4}$, which is sung with the ordinary [i.e. even] tactus, that is three SM to the downstroke and three to the upstroke, and the rests correspond to this tactus." [16] Scaletta's last statement means that two S rests per tactus are used in $C\frac{6}{4}$ just as they are in C; one S rest therefore has the duration of three M, and in order to express a rest the length of one S, two M rests must be used. The following excerpt from a song by Visconti illustrates the shift from $C\frac{3}{2}$ to $\frac{6}{4}$, which results in the same meter taken just twice as fast:

---

15. *Ibid.*, p. 29. "La Meliola si può segnare sotto qualsivoglia Tempo & è quella che manda tre Minime nere a Battuta due in terra & una in aria, & s'usa di farla come dimostrera l'essempio, & ogni volta che non seguirà il tre uscira fuori di Meliola, la quale puo uscire tanto in nere, quanto in bianche.

16. H. Scaletta, *Scala di Musica*, p. 16. "Et in questi tempi moderni vi è ancora la Sesquiquarta la quale si canta sotto la battuta ordinaria, cioè tre nel battere, & tre nel levare, & le Pause giuste à detta battuta."

EX. 7

VISCONTI *p.16*

Prolations

> *Prolationi* are ordinarily used in these two *tempi*, ⊙ and Ͼ; the first calls for perfect prolation in *tempo perfetto*, the second in *tempo imperfetto*. These *prolationi* signify that three M go to a tactus, as they do in *proportione minore*, and they observe the same perfections and alterations as in that *proportione*. The rests of the perfect prolation in *tempo imperfetto* are the same as in the above-mentioned *proportione*, but in the perfect prolation in *tempo perfetto* they are different in that the rest that touches three lines of the staff equals six tactus and the rest that touches two lines equals three. . . . In these *prolatione* are found white *crome*, of which there are six to the tactus; they have the same value as if they were SM in *proportione minore*. . . . Black S and M are used to prevent perfection and alteration; these notes cannot be perfect or altered.[17]

A canzonetta by Bucchianti illustrates most of the peculiarities of the perfect *prolatione:*

EX. 8

BUCCHIANTI *p.18*

17. Brunelli, *op. cit.*, p. 30. "Le Prolationi s'usono ordinariamente in questi due Tempi posti come qui ⊙, Ͼ, il primo Tempo si domanda Prolatione perfetta in Tempo perfetto. La

It is important to note that barlines have no effect upon the rules of perfection and alteration. In the third bar of the soprano two M appear between two S, so the first S (f″) is perfect and the second M (d″) is altered. In the seventh bar black notes are used to prevent the M (e♭) in the bass from being altered, since it is the second of two M between two S. The final note of the solo part requires no dot to be perfect since it is followed by another S at the beginning of the next phrase, whereas in the bass the contrary is the case.

During the sixteenth century the dot in the center of the circle or semicircle of the mensural sign meant perfect prolation but also had an additional significance in that it called for augmentation, in which the value of a complete tactus was given to the M. This usage was discontinued in the seventeenth century, but in order to avoid possible confusion with the former practice, numbers indicating triple proportions were sometimes added to the signs for perfect prolation, thus: Ͼ$^{3}_{1}$, ☉$^{3}_{2}$. Olifante describes perfect prolation as follows:

> [it is] another way of writing *sesquialtera minore* but perfect in respect to prolation which renders the S and its rest perfect. The dot in the center of the sign has no other effect [than to make the S perfect, that is equal to three M, when it follows another S or a rest of the same value]. The above mentioned *tempi* without numbers still usually transfer the tactus to the M; this is commonly called "singing double" [*cantare doppio*]. When the composer desires this [he will use] ☉ or this other sign Ͼ, but if he should then want to go into a *tripla* a number will be placed thus Ͼ $^{3}_{1}$, indicating that where one M was allotted to a tactus there will now be three.[18]

Fortunately this cumbersome device, which calls for augmentation and then immediately cancels it, is not of frequent occurrence. As a matter of fact

---

seconda si domanda Prolatione perfetta in Tempo imperfetto. Le quali Prol. significano che vanno tre Minime à battuta, & nell'istesso modo, che si canta la Proportione minore & s'osservano tutte le Perfetioni, & Alterationi, che in detta Proportione si trovano, & le Pause nella Prol. perf, in Tempo imperfetto vanno ordinariamente, & si cantano nel medesimo modo della Proportione sopradetta. E nella Prolatione perfetta in Tempo perfetto vanno altrimenti cioè le Pause che toccano tre righe vagliono sei. Et le Pause che toccano due righe vagliono tre . . . In dette Prolationi si trovano le Crome bianche delle quali ne vanno sei à battuta, che varranno a essere come fossero Semiminime in Proportione minore, & in dette prolatione tanto vagliono le Semiminime quanto le Crome bianche. La Semibreve & Minime nere sono fatte per levare le perfezioni & Alterationi le quali Note non possono essere perfette, ne alterate."

18. Olifante, *Trattato Brevissimo*, p. 120. "Alio modo di note minori, ma perfetto rispetto dalla prolatione quale fa perfetta la semibreve e sue pause, il cui officio del punto posto in mezzo del segno non fa altro effetto. . . . Li sopradetti tempi ancora senza zifra si suol mandare la minima in una battuta, e si dice volgarmente cantar doppio. Allhora quando cosi vorrà il Compositore, òvero à quest' altro tempo Ͼ ma si poi volesse entrare nella tripla, la zifra vuol signata cosi $^{3}_{1}$ dicendo ove ne mandavi una minima in una battuta ne vadano tre."

perfect prolations are not common in the Italian sources of this period, having been replaced in general use by *proportione minore* or *sesquialtera*, both of which have practically identical results.

Incomplete Signatures

BRUNELLI CONCLUDES his treatment of *proportioni*, *sesquialtera*, and *emiolia* with a warning that they must be indicated in the way he has done and with the same tempo signs, for "otherwise errors would arise because the numbers would not show the correct values and everything would be confused and misunderstood." [19] Unfortunately other composers, scribes, and even theorists were not as conscientious as Brunelli, and one or another aspect of the signature is frequently left to be inferred from whatever is given. Numbers, for instance, often appear at the beginning of a piece without any tempo sign, so that the latter must be deduced from the note values that are used. Scaletta gives the sign $\frac{3}{2}$ for *sesquialtera maggiore*, omitting the C and defining it as "that which is made up of B and S and is sung with three S to the tactus." [20] For *sesquialtera minore* he gives simply 3 as a signature, explaining that it is composed of S and M and is sung with three M to the tactus. Such partial signatures are not rare in the musical sources, especially in manuscripts, for scribes tended to be less scrupulous than editors of printed editions. The most common partial sign is C3, which appears frequently in the Barbera MS as well as in Magl. XIX, 25 and 66. If interpreted literally the 3 should stand for $\frac{3}{1}$, which according to the rule of numbers should mean three S per tactus. The contexts sometimes show, however, that this is not the meaning intended and that C3 often stands for *sesquialtera minore* (three M per tactus), the denominator 2 being omitted. This is usually also the significance of the simple number 3 when it appears in the course of a piece that has started in C.

Conclusions

ARMED WITH the information summarized in this chapter, we should be able to reconstruct on a strictly mathematical basis the relative durations of notes under each signature and to coordinate these durations in the correct

19. Brunelli, *op. cit.*, p. 29.
20. Scaletta, *op. cit.*, p. 16.

relationship to a regular unit of time. We have learned, moreover, that the tactus is always divided into two parts, which are sometimes equal and sometimes unequal (the first part being twice the length of the second), and that the notation shows which type of tactus is intended for each case. Further information on the relative speed of the tactus under various signatures gives us some clues in regard to tempo. A mechanically correct and "authentic" rendition of the notes should therefore be possible through observation of the rules.

For a rhythmical—that is to say, a *musical*—performance of these works, however, we need information of a different order: we need to know the kinds of beats, the position of the thetic beats, the constitution of the true measures, the prevailing level of meter, and the points of rhythmic climax. None of these metric and rhythmic facts is explicitly indicated in the notation.

In the face of this anomaly several questions may arise in the mind of the reader, depending on his temperament and experience: (1)Do these so-called "metric and rhythmic facts" actually exist in the performance of the music? Are they not rather products of the imagination—subjective impressions existing only in the mind of the listener? (2)If the latter is true, would not these subjective impressions be aroused automatically through a mechanically correct performance? An affirmative answer to these questions amounts to stating that there is no difference between the musical performance of an inspired artist and that of a well-regulated machine. With people who hold this view no further discussion is possible.

Assuming, on the other hand, that the rhythmic facts referred to actually *do* exist in performance and did exist at the time of origin of the music we are investigating, yet are *not* explicitly indicated in the notation, must we therefore give up any attempt to recapture them for our own use? Or are there other, indirect methods of approach? We are dealing, perhaps, with imponderables. But even imponderables can be approached (though not "captured," in the strict sense of the word) through subtle and devious routes. The following points, it seems to me, deserve consideration before we abandon the attempt to discover the true rhythm of seventeenth-century music:

1. The tactus, though it does not specify a particular meter, is not entirely unrelated to meter, for only a limited number of meters are compatible with a given type of tactus. In other words, the tactus does not tell us *which* meter is intended, but it does limit the possibilities. A detailed exploration of this relationship between tactus and meter will be the subject of the next Chapter.

2. In the case of dance music, the steps and figures of individual dances impose certain limitations on the music: a certain kind of beat at a certain tempo, with articulations, at predetermined intervals, and points of emphasis on certain beats. The effect of these limitations and the patterns of musical rhythm that spring from them will be investigated in Chapter IV.

3. Similarly, in the case of vocal music the prosody of the text suggests definite points of repose, emphasis, and articulation. If the composer has respected the prosody, the points of repose, emphasis, and articulation in the music will coincide with them. Chapter V will be devoted to an attempt to identify patterns of musical rhythm that are derived from settings of verse texts.

4. The harmony often defines the position of thetic beats. A clear harmonic cadence indicates the appropriate placement of a barline, and it is not difficult to discover whether the beats included between barlines are divisible by two or by three.

5. Certain configurations of note values suggest certain meters and rhythmic patterns; while they are often subject to various interpretations, they limit the number of possibilities.

6. Each period and style in the history of music has its own vocabulary of rhythms. This is especially true of the Baroque era, one of the characteristic features of which is the use of stereotyped rhythmic patterns. Once a pattern has been identified, it is fairly easy to recognize its recurrence.

THREE

THE RELATION OF TACTUS TO METER

IN ORDER TO IDENTIFY AND DEFINE THE VARIOUS TYPES OF RHYTHMIC PATTERNS of the early seventeenth century, our first requirement is information concerning the metrical bases of these patterns. Once we have established the kinds of beats and the constitutions of the true measures, the other rhythmic features, such as the lengths of units and the points of climax, can more easily be determined. We have seen that the notation gives us definite information regarding the note values used under the various time signatures and the manner in which these are related to a regular unit of time called the tactus, but that it does not always specify how the pulses represented by the note values are to be grouped into beats or how the beats are to be organized into measures. The number of metrical groupings compatible with each time signature and with each of the two kinds of tactus, however, is limited. Our investigation of early seventeenth-century meters will begin with an exploration of these potential groupings.

Tactus Aequalis

THE TACTUS, as described by the theorists of the early sixteenth century (e.g. Ornithoparcus [1519] and Agricola [1532]) was essentially equivalent to the concept we have described as the beat. The prevailing movement being in minims, each minim was felt as a pulse and was represented by a motion of the hand, each downstroke corresponding to the thesis and each upstroke to the arsis of the beat, which was equivalent to the value of a semibreve, according to the normal tactus under the signature C. With the increasing use of smaller note values during the sixteenth century, the minim was often subdivided consistently throughout a piece. When this occurred, the minim took on the quality of a beat, *its* subdivisions (semiminims) being perceived as pulses. In some pieces even the semiminim became the primary beat, because of a prevailing motion in *crome* (eighth notes). The tactus, however, remained identified with the value of a semibreve, and when barlines were introduced in the seventeenth century they were most often placed at intervals corresponding to the duration of the tactus (the semibreve) even though they embraced two or more beats. This gave rise to an immense confusion of terminology which has not yet been straightened out. The Italian word for tactus, *battuta*, means literally "beat," but is now commonly used for the space between two barlines, or "measure" in the modern sense. The German word *Takt* and the French word *mesure* went through similar changes, which are especially misleading since all these words acquired, during the Classic period, metrical connotations that they originally did not have.

The downstroke and the upstroke of the tactus must be regarded as ticks of a metronome, each of which may be mentally subdivided once or twice, the subdivisions corresponding to pulses. Thus the even tactus indicated by the signs C or ₵ may contain two, four, or eight pulses which when grouped by twos may be perceived as one semibreve beat, two minim beats, or four semiminim beats respectively. Furthermore, since there is no metrical distinction between the downstroke and the upstroke of the tactus, nothing prevents the six pulses contained in one-and-a-half tactus from forming three groups of two semiminims or two groups of three semiminims. Three even tactus under the sign C may therefore refer to:

1. Three measures of two 𝅗𝅥 beats each.
2. Two measures of three 𝅗𝅥 beats each.
3. Two measures of two 𝅗𝅥. beats each.
4. Six measures of two 𝅘𝅥 beats each.
5. Four measures of three 𝅘𝅥 beats each.

The following Table, which expresses these meters in terms of common present-day time signatures, may further clarify the possible interpretations of three even tactus of seventeenth-century notation:

TABLE II

Tactus	1		2		3	
	↓	↑	↓	↑	↓	↑
C	𝅗𝅥	𝅗𝅥	𝅗𝅥	𝅗𝅥	𝅗𝅥	𝅗𝅥

	Meter	
1.	C or $\frac{4}{4}$	♩ ♩ ♩ ♩ | ♩ ♩ ♩ ♩ | ♩ ♩ ♩ ♩
2.	$\frac{3}{2}$	♩ ♩ ♩ ♩ ♩ ♩ | 𝅗𝅥 𝅗𝅥 𝅗𝅥
3.	$\frac{6}{4}$	𝅗𝅥 ♩ 𝅗𝅥 ♩ | 𝅗𝅥. 𝅗𝅥.
4.	$\frac{2}{4}$	♫ ♫ | ♫ ♫ | ♩ ♩ | ♫ ♫ | ♫ ♫ | ♩ ♩
5.	$\frac{3}{4}$	♫ ♫ ♫ | ♫ ♫ ♫ | ♩ ♩ ♩ | ♩ ♩ ♩

This Table does not include all the mathematical possibilities, but only the combinations that occur fairly frequently in the musical sources. Under the sign for *tempo minore imperfetto*, ₵, where if performed correctly the tactus corresponds to the breve, two further possibilities may be added; namely, our series of six minims could indicate three duple beats (3𝅝.) or two triple beats (2𝅝.) and correspond to a single measure of $\frac{3}{1}$ or $\frac{6}{2}$. The other two *tempi* (O and Φ) would cause no alteration in the chart, since in both cases the tactus = S, as in C.

It is true, perhaps, that the sign C most often represents two duple beats per measure, as in meter No. 1; but the indiscriminate transcription of all pieces bearing this signature into $\frac{4}{4}$ time has obscured many triple meters of the types 2 and 3. Furthermore, the constitution of the measure is often misrepresented through failure to take into account that the downstroke of the tactus does not necessarily coincide with the first beat of a measure. There are actually several variants to meters No. 1 and No. 2, according to whether the rhythm begins on a thetic or arsic beat or part of a beat. The following examples will illustrate some of these possibilities. The original notation is reproduced, including barlines when present, with the addition of arrows indicating the tactus. The true measures are shown by the dotted barlines, and their constitution in number and value of beats is given in parentheses, e.g. (3𝅗𝅥) = a measure of $\frac{3}{2}$ time; (3 × 3𝅗𝅥) = 3 measures of $\frac{2}{3}$ time; (3 × 2𝅗𝅥) = 3 measures of C, etc.

EXAMPLE 9. Meter No. 1, beginning with the arsis of a beat. All pieces are written as though they begin on the first downstroke of the tactus. If the first note (or notes) falls on the arsis of a beat, this is usually indicated by a rest in the original notation; but then the first thesis inevitably coincides with the *upstroke* of the tactus, so that all subsequent barring according to tactus is wrong in relation to the thetic beat of the true measure.

EX. 9

Meter No. 1 BARBERA *fol.49*

EXAMPLE 10. The phrase begins with an arsis of half a beat, as indicated by the semiminim rest. Accents fall on the penultimate syllables of A*mo*re and *mi*ri, causing syncopations in bars 2 and 4. As in the previous example, the thetic beats of the true measures coincide with the upstroke of the tactus.

EX. 10

Meter No. 1 BARBERA *fols.35, 67*

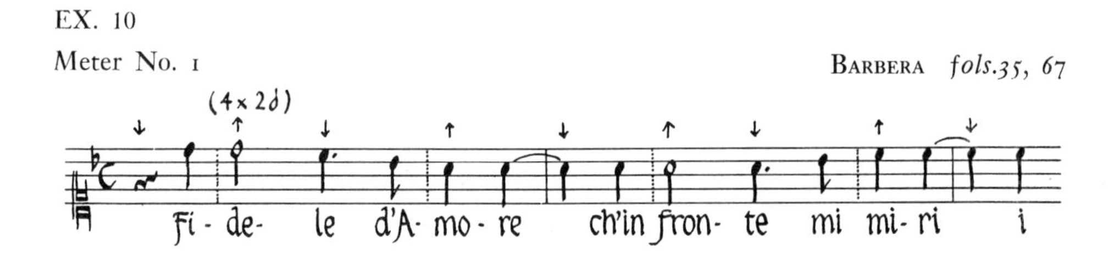

EXAMPLE 11. The prevailing movement in *crome* (eighth notes) implies a semiminim beat, which could well be transcribed as modern $\frac{2}{4}$ meter. It could also be interpreted as $\frac{4}{4}$, omitting every other barline. In either case the barlines should be readjusted to accommodate the arsic beginning of the phrase.

EX. 11

Meter No. 4 BRUNELLI, 1616 *p.13*

Example 12 is in meter No. 2, as shown by the accents on the third syllable of risve*glia*tevi and the penultimates of Pa*sto*ri and *can*to and also suggested by the disposition of the longer note values. It will be noted that in a series of triple measures in which the beat = ½ tactus, the first beat of every other measure necessarily coincides with the upstroke of the tactus.

EX. 12

Meter No. 2 — Magl. xix, 25 *fol.21*

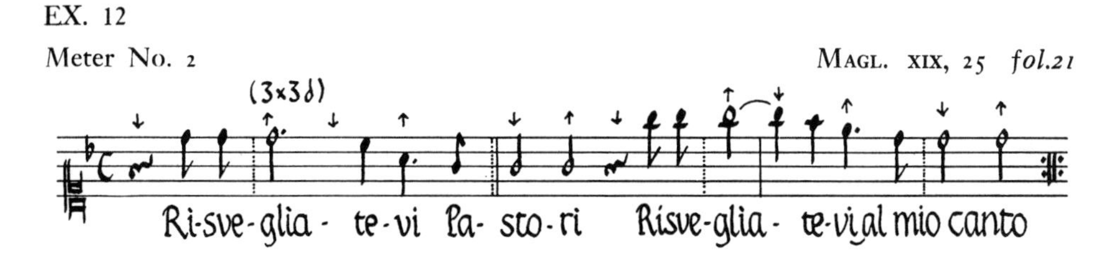

Example 13. The prevailing movement indicates minim beats. The positions of the thetic beats should coincide with the accented penultimates of the feminine verse endings ar*cie*re, *ne*re, and a*mo*re. The beats should therefore be grouped in threes, producing meter No. 2, or $\frac{3}{2}$ time. The phrase begins with two arsic beats, so the first of the original barlines is correct but the others must be readjusted.

EX. 13

Meter No. 2 — G. B. Gagliano *p.9*

Example 14 shows the alternation of meters No. 3 and No. 2, corresponding to the modern $\frac{6}{4}$ and $\frac{3}{2}$ meters, or more properly, $\frac{6}{8}$ and $\frac{3}{4}$ with reduced note values—the characteristic hemiola rhythm. It is interesting to note that these two triple meters are in this case notated under the supposedly duple signature, C.

EX. 14

Meter Nos. 3 and 2 — Brunelli, 1614 *p.1*

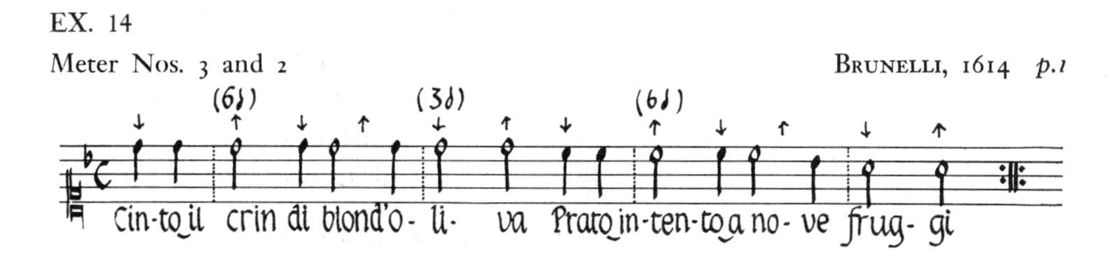

EXAMPLE 15. Meter No. 1 begins regularly, coinciding with the tactus, but the arsic beginning of the third phrase and the obligatory accent on the first syllable of *spen*to causes a shift to meter No. 2, requiring the insertion of a $\frac{3}{2}$ measure.

EX. 15
Meter Nos. 1 and 2 — BARBERA *fol.25*

Tactus Inaequalis

SINCE THE uneven tactus used in the *proportioni*, *sesquialtera*, and *emiolia* was expressly devised to govern the performance of three notes in the time of two, or in some cases in the time of one, it may be assumed that under normal conditions the three notes are to be grouped together and, therefore, that the uneven tactus refers to a triple beat. The large number and variety of signatures demanding this tactus do not imply a corresponding number and variety of meters. The profusion of time signatures in use at this time did not arise through concern for metrical problems; it was rather the result of experimental attempts to establish precise temporal relationships between this tactus and the standard tactus of *tempo maggiore imperfetto* (C). The experiments were doomed to failure because, even at this time, the "standard" tactus was no longer standard and became less and less so during the course of the seventeenth century.

In contrast to the variety of possible meters notated under the single sign C, we now encounter a variety of possible ways of notating a single meter. So, instead of compiling a table of possible meters for one notation, it will be more profitable to compile a table of possible notations for one meter. Let us take, for example, four triple beats grouped in twos; that is, two measures of "compound time" such as might be expressed in modern notation as

$\frac{6}{4}$ 𝅗𝅥 ♩𝅗𝅥♩ | 𝅗𝅥. 𝅗𝅥. (2 x 2 𝅗𝅥.) or $\frac{6}{8}$ ♩♪♩♪ | ♩. ♩. (2 x 2 ♩.)

TABLE III

	Tactus	1 ↓	1 ↑	2 ↓	2 ↑	3 ↓	3 ↑	4 ↓	4 ↑
Sesquialtera maggiore or Tripla	$¢\frac{3}{2}$ or $C\frac{3}{1}$	⊟	◇	⊟	◇	⊟·		⊟·	
Proportione maggiore	$\Phi\frac{3}{2}$ or $O\frac{3}{1}$	⊟	◇	⊟	◇	⊟		⊟·	
Sesquialtera minore	$C\frac{3}{2}$	◇	◇ with stem	◇	◇ with stem	◇·		◇·	
Proportione minore or *Prolatione perfetta*	$O\frac{3}{2}$ C[$C\frac{3}{1}$ $O\frac{3}{2}$]	◇	◇ with stem	◇	◇ with stem	◇		◇·	
Sesquiquarta	$C\frac{6}{4}$	◇ ◆◇	◆	◇· ◇·					
Emiolia maggiore	¢	■	◆	■	◆	■·		■·	
Emiolia minore	C	◆	◆ with stem	◆	◆ with stem	◆·		◆·	

To these must be added the incomplete signatures C 3 and 3, which leave the performer to deduce from the context *which* notes are to be grouped in threes to correspond to the unequal tactus.

The Table contains one example—the sesquiquarta, $C\frac{6}{4}$—which, strictly speaking, does not belong to the same category as the others, since it was performed to an even tactus. It seemed best to include it here in order to discuss the signatures that unequivocally call for a triple beat at the same time. All the versions shown in the Table except the $C\frac{6}{4}$ were performed to four uneven tactus. The signatures do not, however, specify the constitution of the measures, since in each case the tactus corresponds to the beat, and we have defined measure as a grouping of beats. A measure of triple beats can be expressed in modern notation only through what we call compound meter. Although the $C\frac{6}{4}$ was the only signature in use in the early seventeenth century that specifically called for compound meter, there is no reason to believe that the other tactus-beats were not also grouped in twos or threes in actual performance. The distinction is one of tempo rather than meter; the four beats of $C\frac{6}{4}$ occupy only two tactus instead of four, so they obviously must move faster. In the musical sources of the last half of the seventeenth century there is a sharp increase in the number of numerical signs used to denote compound meters; we find not only $\frac{6}{8}$, $\frac{9}{8}$, and $\frac{12}{8}$, but also many signatures that are no longer in use today, such as $\frac{9}{4}$, $\frac{9}{16}$, $\frac{6}{16}$, and $\frac{12}{16}$. These signatures are enumerated and described in the theoretical works published during the last half of the century, e.g. G. M. Bononcini's *Musico prattico* (1673) and L. Penna's *Li primi albori musicali* (1672). There is no reason to suppose that all the meters and rhythmic patterns designated by these signs were completely new phenomena, appearing suddenly for the first time in the art of music. It is far more likely that many of the new signs represent new methods of notating, and probably also of conducting, the meters that had heretofore been implied by the various types of *tripla* shown in the above Table. We are therefore quite justified in transcribing these in compound meters whenever we find evidence of the grouping of beats by twos or by threes.

It is true that the meters represented in Table III may be, and in modern editions usually are, transcribed into $\frac{2}{3}$ or $\frac{3}{4}$ measures. Such transcriptions are, however, just as noncommittal as the seventeenth-century notation, in that they show only one level of meter. This comparison serves to point to a deficiency in our modern notation: namely, that our "measures" of $\frac{3}{2}$ or $\frac{3}{4}$, when they represent a *single* beat—that is, when the half notes or quarter notes, respectively, are not subdivided—are not really measures at all, if we hold to our definition of a measure as a *group* of beats.

If the notes shown in Table III should be subdivided by the insertion of smaller note values, the series might be perceived as representing twelve duple beats on the next lower level; that is, with six pulses to each tactus instead of three. In this case, a transcription into $\frac{3}{2}$ or $\frac{3}{4}$ measures would be legitimate, in that each measure would represent a group of three duple beats. The organization on the higher level, that of the grouping of the tactus, however, would be lost or at least obscured.

In certain kinds of pieces, notably gagliardas, two levels of meter are present and should be perceptible to the listener or dancer. It is not always possible to suggest the two levels simultaneously in our notation, but a compound measure is more likely to do so than a simple measure. To illustrate this problem, let us examine a gagliarda which Brunelli published in both a simple vocal version and an instrumental ornamented version. Example 16 shows four beats of the simple version, presented originally without barlines. The context of the text and of the dance shows that the measure organization is 1 + 2 + 1, as indicated in the dotted barlines. Example 17 shows the same four beats in the original instrumental version, with barlines placed according to tactus. A transcription in $\frac{3}{4}$ as in Example 18, with reduced note values, would be correct, but a transcription of both versions in $\frac{6}{4}$ (Examples 19 and 20) would have the advantage of indicating a thesis on beats 2 and 4 of the higher level (beat = 𝅗𝅥.) or 4 and 10 of the lower level (beat = ♩).

Hemiola

MENTION MUST be made of the *hemiola* meter that is so characteristic of the Baroque era. It consists of the alternation of a measure of 2 triple beats and a measure of 3 duple beats or vice versa, similar to an alternation of $\frac{6}{8}$ and $\frac{3}{4}$ or of $\frac{6}{4}$ and $\frac{3}{2}$ in modern terms. We have already seen (Ex. 14 above) that such an alternation was sometimes notated under the plain signature C without any express indication of the shift even though it involved a polyrhythmic conflict between the tactus and the beat. In pieces that were written to be performed with an unequal tactus, on the other hand, there was often, though not always, a definite indication of the change of meter, presumably because the unequal tactus normally implies a triple beat whereas the equal tactus of C made no implication one way or the other. The indication took the form of black notes. As Brunelli observed, black notes are always imperfect and are used in perfect *tempi* to prevent perfection and alteration. Three black notes, then, are to be performed in the time of two perfect white notes. Since the unequal tactus normally stands for a perfect note, the 3 black notes are performed in the time of 2 unequal tactus, changing the meter from 2 triple beats to 3 duple beats in spite of polyrhythmic conflict again involved between tactus and beat.

The following examples show four ways of expressing the hemiola meter:

1. (Ex. 21) Four tactus of *sesquialtera maggiore*, with black notes for the three duple beats.

2. (Ex. 22) Four tactus of *sesquialtera minore*, with black notes in the bass and white notes in the soprano.

3. (Ex. 23) Two tactus of *sesquialtera minore*, with the hemiola occurring on the level of minims instead of semibreves.

4. (Ex. 24) Two tactus of *sesquiquarta*. All four examples might be

transcribed: $\frac{6}{4}$ 𝅗𝅥 ♩ 𝅗𝅥 ♩ | $\frac{3}{2}$ 𝅗𝅥 𝅗𝅥 𝅗𝅥 but the last two naturally demand a faster tempo, since, assuming the tactus to be approximately the same speed, they are to be performed in half the time.

Changes of Signature

Finally we must consider the effect upon meter of signature changes during the course of a single piece. It should be evident from the discussion so far that change of meter and change of signature are by no means synonymous. We have seen examples of changes of meter under the even tactus, C, with no indication in the notation that the change should take place. We have also seen examples of changes of meter under the uneven tactus (hemiola) with and without special indications but with no change of signature.

It must be remembered that meter has two elements, beats and measures, and that a change in (1) the kind of beat—duple to triple, or vice versa, (2) in the constitution of the measure (number of beats grouped together), or (3) in both, must be regarded as a change of meter. The question arises as to whether a change of signature always involves a change of meter, and, if so, what is the nature of the change. Furthermore, since different signatures have different implications in regard to tempo, we must take cognizance of the possibility that a change of signature may also indicate a change of tempo.

Let us consider, first, a case in which the change of signature results *only* in a change of tempo, the meter remaining the same but proceeding at a different speed. We have already encountered such a case in the last Chapter, but since this aspect of it was not dealt with at the time, the example may be repeated here and discussed in greater detail. In Visconti's *Non vuoi che t'ami* there occurs the following passage:

EX. 25

Visconti *p.16*

At first sight this appears to be a simple case of hemiola, wherein the value of the semiminims remains constant but their grouping changes from three times two (three minims in the measures before the $\frac{6}{4}$) to two times three (two dotted minims in the measures following the $\frac{9}{4}$). From a strictly mathematical point of view this is true, but this interpretation fails to take into account that the phrase in C $\frac{3}{2}$ actually implies a compound measure on a higher level of meter than that of the phrase in $\frac{6}{4}$. In other words the pulse is represented in the first phrase by the minim, in the second by the semiminim, so that the meter consists of measures of two triple beats both before and after the change of signature; the only difference is that after the change the two triple beats are exactly twice as fast. This, in my opinion, constitutes a change of tempo. In performance the conductor, or the soloist, conducting himself mentally, should give two 𝅗𝅥. beats per measure for the first phrase and two ♩. beats per measure for the second, as indicated in reduced note values in Example 26.

EX. 26

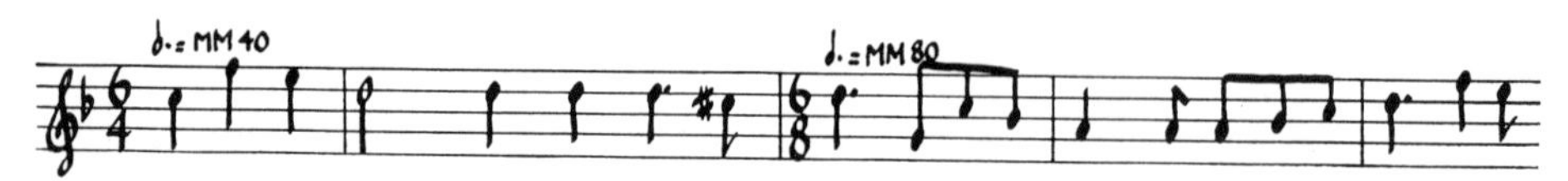

The same effect would be produced if the whole passage were written in minims and semiminims without change of signature but with an indication to double the tempo for the second phrase.

This example illustrates an important principle of musical interpretation that is often disregarded, particularly in present-day performances of early music. Whenever a theme appears in diminution a change of tempo is involved, whether or not a different time signature is present in the score. If the performer does not feel a faster beat the true meter will be distorted, and the relationship between the theme and its diminution will be obscured. The example serves also to clarify the distinction between the tactus and the musical beat and to point out one difference between a mathematically correct performance and a musical one.

One should not lose sight of the fact that the change of tempo in *Non vuoi che t'ami* is no mere technical subtlety but was inserted to produce a specific effect. The line "E tu l'ingrata, la dispietata," which recurs with different adjectives in each stanza of the text, takes on a particular force through being sung twice as fast as the previous line. This is only one of many ways in which composers of the time made use of a few more or less stereotyped rhythmic patterns, modifying them in various ways to suit the context of the individual composition.

A favorite expressive device of early Baroque composers is what might be called "metric variation": the repetition in duple beats of a pattern that has first been stated in triple beats, or the repetition in measures of three beats of a pattern first stated in measures of two beats. In this connection the following excerpts containing changes of time signature may profitably be examined with respect to the resulting changes in meter and tempo:

EXAMPLE 27, from Visconti's *Cruda Filli*, illustrates both of the above-mentioned types of metric variation. The excerpt consists of three phrases, the first of which proceeds in measures of two triple beats, the second in measures of two duple beats and the third in measures of three duple beats. The shift from triple to duple beats is indicated by the change of signature from $\frac{6}{4}$ to C; the change of measure from two to three duple beats is not specified in the notation. The transcription into modern notation of the first change presents a problem for which I have found no completely satisfactory solution. In order to clarify the manner in which this change comes about

EX. 27

VISCONTI *p.8*

Example 27b shows the whole passage as it would be sung in triple beats throughout; this may be compared with Example 27c, which shows the passage in duple beats, both with reduced note values. It will be noted that if the second phrase is to be sung in duple beats the meter must change in the middle of a measure. Modern notation has no way of indicating a measure containing a triple beat and a duple beat except by placing a triplet sign over the triple beat. But if we do this the entire first phrase will have to be notated in triplets. This, however, would give the impression that the basic meter of the piece is in duple beats, which is not the case. The only solution I can propose is to divide the transition measure into two measures, one of one triple beat ($\frac{3}{8}$) and another of one duple beat ($\frac{2}{4}$) with an indication that the half note in the second has the same value as the dotted quarter in the first (Ex. 27d).

EXAMPLE 28, *Ladra d'amore* by G. B. da Gagliano, contains another instance of metric variation. In this case the second phrase, in duple beats, proceeds on a lower level of meter than the first, so that whatever value is assigned to the triple beat of the first phrase (a dotted semibreve in the original) must be divided in two to represent the duple beat of the second phrase. The change is further complicated by the fact that the transition measure should include the upbeat of the second phrase and thus should consist of: a triple beat, two duple beats which together equal the value of that triple beat, a third duple beat representing the arsis of the next phrase. A change in tempo is obviously involved here, and would probably be easier to effect after the last note of the first phrase than during that note. In the proposed transcription, therefore (Ex. 28b), the note sung to the last syllable of *core* is incorporated into the $\frac{6}{4}$ measure, the arsis of the second phrase is given a measure of $\frac{2}{4}$ and the relation of the half note to the preceding dotted half note is indicated by a metronome mark, which, however, is not intended to specify an absolute tempo.

EX. 28

G. B. GAGLIANO *p.18*

EXAMPLE 29, from a spiritual madrigal by Marco da Gagliano, shows several changes of meter. At the appearance of the sign C the beat changes from triple to duple. The five tactus under C divide into two equal parts, 2½ + 2½, at the cadence on *piè*. These parts correspond to 2 𝅗𝅥 + 3 𝅗𝅥 and 3 𝅗𝅥 + 2 𝅗𝅥 respectively. The semibreve on *sù* prepares the shift to a lower level of meter, that is, the beat = 𝅗𝅥 instead of 𝅝. The passage under the signature C therefore contains a $\frac{2}{4}$ measure, two $\frac{3}{4}$ measures, and another $\frac{2}{4}$ measure, as shown in Example 29b.

EX. 29

M. GAGLIANO *p.27*

EXAMPLE 30. Domenico Brunetti's setting of four short lines of text changes from measures of two triple beats to measures of two duple beats and back again. In transcription the extra duple beat on the final syllable of cand*ore* can be incorporated into the $\frac{6}{4}$ measure since the semibreve on that cadence tone is the same length as the three minims that form the arsis of the final phrase (Ex. 30b).

EX. 30

MAGL. XIX, 25 *fol.8ᵛ*

EXAMPLE 31a is from a dance tune called *La Barriera* by Cesare Negri, and Example 31b is from his lute accompaniment to the same dance, written in tablature; there can therefore be no doubt as to their metrical equivalence. The melody is written with the signature 3 without barlines, whereas the tablature has no signature but is barred regularly. In neither version is there any indication of the change of meter at the repeat sign. The dance shows that both phrases are of the same length and contain the same number of beats, and the barring by tactus in the lute version shows that the beats are triple before the repeat sign and duple after it. According to Brunelli's rule the signature of the melody should be C^3_2—*sesquialtera minore*—to specify three minims per tactus. The three semiminims per tactus in the lute version are apparently used in the same way as Brunelli's *meliola*, but with no signs to indicate this. The excerpt is transcribed in Example 31c.

EX. 31

NEGRI *pp.123–24*

EXAMPLE 32, the beginning of the first-violin part of a *Zoppa* for four strings by Zanetti, is one of many instances of a very loose application of *meliola*, the number 3 being equivalent to the modern sign for a triplet. Instead of being placed before each group of three notes as Brunelli advises, however, the 3 comes between the second and third notes of each group. After the first three times the 3 no longer appears, but the triplet figure is taken for granted throughout the piece at each recurrence of the dotted semiminim pattern, presumably to accompany the *zoppetto* step of the dance. The other string parts—alto, tenor, and bass—which do not contain triplets, show that there are *two* groups of three semiminims per tactus, not *one* as in the previous example, so that in the transcription (Exx. 32b and c) a beat of the triple meter is equal to one beat of the $\frac{2}{4}$ measure instead of the whole measure.

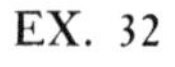
EX. 32

ZANETTI *pp.12–13*

Conclusions

The following conclusions bearing upon the transcription of music of the early seventeenth century into appropriate modern notation may be drawn from our observations of the relation between tactus and meter:

1. The signs C and ¢ in the sources stand for duple meters that may be transcribed as $\frac{4}{4}$, $\frac{2}{4}$, $\frac{2}{2}$, C or ¢, and also for all those triple meters with three slow beats per measure that would now be indicated by $\frac{3}{2}$, slow $\frac{3}{4}$, or even slow $\frac{6}{4}$ when it stands for six slow beats per measure. The choice of the most appropriate meter for a given case, and the decision whether changes from duple meter to slow triple meter (or vice versa) are necessary must be based upon considerations that are not explicit in the notation.

Willi Apel points out that "The practice of using even meter, or, at least barlines suggestive thereof for pieces which from the musical point of view are indubitably in ternary rhythm, persisted long into the seventeenth century." [1] Nevertheless, many editors have been reluctant to use triple time signatures and to change the barlines in passages marked C or ¢ in the original sources. It appears to be hard for them to believe that with so many triple signatures at their disposal composers should still have persisted in using signs for duple meter when they meant triple. The occasional instances in which the structure of the music leaves no doubt that triple meter was intended have been regarded as exceptions or as the result of faulty copying.[2]

It must now be recognized that this manner of writing was neither exceptional nor erroneous but was the standard practice for at least the first half of the seventeenth century. It was, indeed, the *only* means available for notating a slow triple meter, since all triple signatures called for one beat per tactus and there was a limit to how slow the tactus could be taken.[3]

---

1. Cf. Willi Apel, *The Notation of Polyphonic Music*, Cambridge, Mass., 1944.

2. G. Benvenuti, for instance, in the appendix to his transcription of the 1609 edition of Monteverdi's *Orfeo*, makes the following statement: "The text of the original score has four minims per measure, and it may be said that the barline is placed indiscriminately to separate the four beats. This would seem rather to be the work of a person ignorant of music, for occasionally the real measures have a different number of beats than those indicated, and the arses and theses fall in different places than those where we see them."

3. The mensural notation of the fifteenth and sixteenth centuries provided several means of indicating slow triple meter that are no longer applicable in the seventeenth century: (1) *Tempus perfectum*, O, while it does not absolutely require semibreves to be grouped by threes at least suggests measures of three tactus, and transcriptions that use this meter usually agree with the musical structure. (2) Similarly, the signs for perfect prolation, ⊙ and Ċ, when used to denote triple augmentation with the minim corresponding to the tactus, suggest a grouping of minims by threes, again resulting in a meter of three tactus per measure. (3) In *tempus perfectum diminutum*, Φ, the semibreve has the value of ½ tactus, and since

2. All signatures containing the number 3, with whatever *tempo* sign they may be combined (C, ₵, O, Φ, or ⊙), call for *tactus inaequalis* and therefore imply a triple beat that moves fast enough to be grouped into a compound measure. These signatures, then, may correspond to any one of the so-called compound meters of modern notation: $\frac{6}{8}, \frac{9}{8}, \frac{12}{8}, \frac{6}{4}, \frac{9}{4},$ etc. In transcribing such passages it is advisable to reduce the note values in order to avoid such unusual time signatures as $\frac{6}{1}, \frac{9}{2}, \frac{12}{2}$.

3. The only unequivocal sign specifying compound meter that was in common use during the first half of the seventeenth century was $\frac{6}{4}$ (or C$\frac{6}{4}$). This sign calls for an even tactus with three quarter notes on the downstroke and three quarter notes on the upstroke. The movement is generally in a tempo that is best suggested by the modern $\frac{6}{8}$ signature. Since all pieces were assumed to begin with the downstroke of the tactus the original notation does not show whether or not the phrase begins with an upbeat of half a measure, so that in transcription the barlines often need to be readjusted.

The occurrence of other numerical signs is rare during this period. When signs such as $\frac{9}{4}, \frac{4}{9}, \frac{12}{8}, \frac{8}{12}$ do appear, for example in Frescobaldi's toccatas and canzoni, they have a purely proportional significance, as explained in Brunelli's rule of numbers. The time values of the notes relative to the basic *tempo* C or ₵ are specified by this rule, but the actual grouping of the beats may depend on other, extra-notational considerations.

4. The hemiola rhythm—the alternation of groups of three duple beats and two triple beats with the pulse remaining constant—may occur under either triple or duple time signatures or may be indicated by the use of black notes. These meters are best transcribed with alternating $\frac{6}{8}$ and $\frac{3}{4}$ time signatures.

5. When time signatures change during the course of a piece the tactus remains relatively constant, though it may shift from even to uneven divisions of the down-and-upstroke. This means that a change in the value of the notes takes place, as opposed to a change in the grouping of notes of the same value. The change of meter that is indicated thus in modern notation:

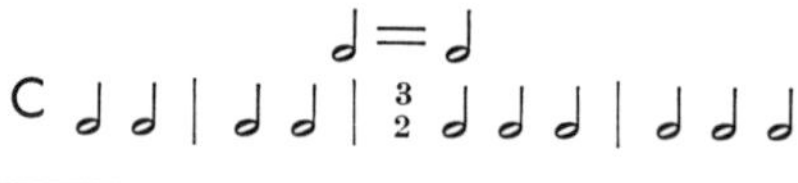

𝅗𝅥 = 𝅗𝅥

C 𝅗𝅥 𝅗𝅥 | 𝅗𝅥 𝅗𝅥 | $\frac{3}{2}$ 𝅗𝅥 𝅗𝅥 𝅗𝅥 | 𝅗𝅥 𝅗𝅥 𝅗𝅥

B = 3 S the normal grouping is three half-tactus per measure. In the seventeenth century these signs for tempus perfectum are described and explained in treatises such as Brunelli's, but have actually been abandoned in practice by all but a few church composers who write in the *stile antico*. The signs O and Φ occur only in conjunction with proportional numbers that force the triple groupings into the duration of a single tactus; they therefore cannot be used to indicate triple groupings of *slow* beats.

is never to be found written this way in the early seventeenth-century Italian sources; the triple grouping of a minim did not require any change in signature since the sign C did not specify duple grouping in the first place. When these two successive signatures *do* occur in the sources of the period, the correct transcription is:

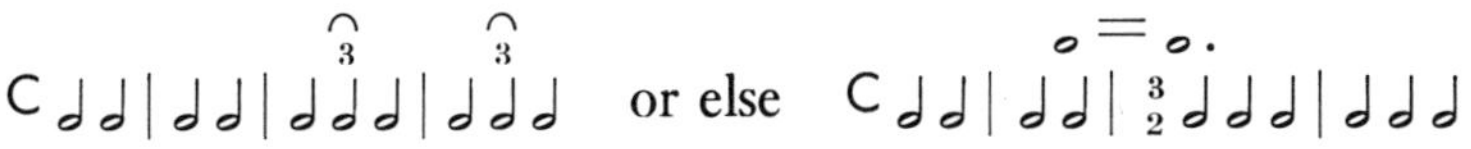

C 𝅗𝅥 𝅗𝅥 | 𝅗𝅥 𝅗𝅥 | 𝅗𝅥 𝅗𝅥 𝅗𝅥 (3) | 𝅗𝅥 𝅗𝅥 𝅗𝅥 (3) or else C 𝅗𝅥 𝅗𝅥 | 𝅗𝅥 𝅗𝅥 | (𝅝 = 𝅝.) $\frac{3}{2}$ 𝅗𝅥 𝅗𝅥 𝅗𝅥 | 𝅗𝅥 𝅗𝅥 𝅗𝅥

FOUR

THE RELATION OF DANCE MOVEMENTS TO MUSICAL RHYTHM

Sources of Information

THE MOST IMPORTANT SOURCE OF INFORMATION CONCERNING THE TECHnique of dancing in the early seventeenth century is a work entitled:

NUOVE/INVENTIONI/DI BALLI,/OPERA VAGHISSIMA/DI CESARE NEGRI MILANESE/DETTO IL TROMBONE,/Famoso, & eccelente Professore di Ballare./*Nella quale si danno i giusti mode del ben portar la vita, & di accommodarsi con ogni*/leggiadria di mouimento ALLE CREANZE, ET GRATIE D'AMORE. Conueneuoli a tutti i CAVALIERE, & DAME, Per ogni sorte di BALLO, BALLETTO, & BRANDO d'Italia, di Spagne, & di Francia./*Con figure bellissime in Rame, & Regole della Musica, & Intavolatura,/quali si richieggono al Suono, & al Canto.*/DIVISA IN TRE TRATTATI/Al Potentissimo, & Catholico/FILIPPO TERZO RE DI SPAGNA Con Privilegio/IN MILANO, Appresso Girolamo Bordone. M. DC. IV.

(New Inventions of Dances, A most beautiful Work by Cesare Negri, called "The Trombonist," Famous and excellent Professor of Dancing. In which are treated the right ways to maintain a proper posture and to follow with ease of movement the "Patterns and Graces of Love." Applicable by all Gentlemen and Ladies to [the dancing of] every sort of Ballo, Balletto, and Brando of Italy, Spain, and France. With most beautiful copper engravings and the Rules for the Music and Tablature that are required for Playing and Singing.

Divided into three Treatises. To the most Powerful and Catholic Philip the Third, King of Spain. With Privilege. In Milan, by Girolamo Bordone, 1604.)

The book is actually a reprint of Negri's *Le Gratie d'Amore*, which had been published two years before by Gio. Battista Piccaglia, Milan, the only change being the substitution of a new title page. One cannot but wonder whether the reason for this change of title may not have been that the extravagant metaphor *Gratie d'Amore*, which may be interpreted "ornaments of [the Court of] Love" or perhaps even "aids to courtship" but which in any case refers to court dancing, proved to be too farfetched to enable prospective customers to grasp what the book was about. The language of the title page, abounding in hyperbole and pompous expressions, is characteristic of Negri's style as well as that of his predecessor, Fabritio Caroso of Sermonetta, who published two works of similar character: *Il Ballarino*, Venice, 1581, and *Nobiltà di Dame*, Venice, 1605. The plethora of technical terms and the stylized phraseology used by both authors present many problems of interpretation to the modern reader. Nevertheless, we cannot agree with Curt Sachs that "Caroso does not know how to explain" or that Negri is "even less satisfactory" and "has little of his own to offer the student." [1] Both Negri and Caroso give such detailed and meticulous descriptions of every step and movement, as well as the precise sequence in which they occur, that it is quite possible, with considerable patience and some imagination, to reconstruct these balli and balletti and to coordinate them with the music. This task has, indeed, already been performed for four of Negri's dances and three of Caroso's by Mabel Dolmetsch in *Dances of Spain and Italy*.[2]

The music that our authors have provided to accompany their dances is not entirely unknown to those who have access to Oscar Chilesotti's *Biblioteca di Rarità Musicali* which has, unfortunately, itself become a rarity. Chilesotti transcribed the dances from the 1605 edition of Caroso's work and 15 of Negri's 43 dance tunes. In doing so, however, he transposed the music up a major sixth, reduced the note values, and changed the time signatures and barlines, so that the modern edition is not suitable for study of the original notation.

Negri's work is the principal source for the present study of the relation between dance movements and musical rhythm. The First Treatise (30 pages) of the three to which he refers in the title lists the celebrated dancers who

1. Curt Sachs, *World History of the Dance*, New York, 1937, p. 345.
2. Mabel Dolmetsch, *Dances of Spain and Italy*, London, 1954.

flourished during the author's lifetime, gives a description of the masquerades and other spectacles in which he took part, and the names of the famous personages whom he had taught and for whom he had danced. The Second Treatise (73 pages) gives 45 rules for executing the steps and movements required in dancing the gagliarda. The Third and most extensive Treatise (194 pages) offers detailed descriptions of 25 steps that are commonly used in balli; numerous modifications of these steps are introduced in the last part of this Treatise, which is devoted to instructions for performing 43 specific balli and balletti.

For the sake of comparison and in order to corroborate the principles derived from the study of Negri, examples will be drawn from other musical sources, some of which have already been cited in Chapter I.

Gasparo Zanetti, *Il Scolaro* (Milan, 1645), ostensibly a treatise on violin playing, is actually an anthology of 70 dances arranged for four string instruments, printed in separate parts in notation without barlines and duplicated in violin tablature. It is interesting to note that Zanetti includes a number of the very same dances that were published 40 years earlier in Negri's treatise. The vogue for saltarelli, gagliarde, and corrente had not abated by mid-century.

Lorenzo Allegri, *Il Primo Libro delle Musiche* (Venice, 1618), contains eight balli written for the court of the Grand Duke of Tuscany and performed at the Pitti Palace or at Pisa between 1608 and 1618. Dances included in the balletti are: gagliarda, corrente, brando, canario, and gavotta.

Antonio Brunelli, *Balletto a 5*, performed at Pisa in 1615, from *Scherzi, Arie, Canzonette e Madrigali*, Libro Terzo (Venice, 1616), contains a ballo grave, gagliarda, and corrente all based on the same melody.

Martino Pesenti, *Ballo sopra la Gagliarda di Cinque Passi*, from *Il quarto libro di Madrigali* (Venice, 1638).

MS Magl. XIX, 31, Biblioteca Nazionale, Florence, a manuscript book of dance instructions containing some of the same dances described by Negri and Caroso.

The Metric Structure of Dance Strains

We shall begin our investigation of the relation between dance patterns and musical rhythm with a study of the formal structure of the dance and of the music that accompanies it. Strictly speaking the term ballo as used in the dance treatises refers to a single dance, while balletto is applied to a suite of contrasting movements that includes, besides the ballo, at least one gagliarda and a choice of other dances such as the corrente, canario, saltarello, and sciolta. Actually, however, the distinction is not rigid, since a ballo often consists of several strains, one of which may be in the rhythm of a gagliarda or corrente. The ballo, as danced, is made up of a number of figures (*parte*), each figure consisting of several steps (*passi*). The dance "step" is not a single motion but a complex of motions that often occupies three, four, or even six or eight beats of music. When the separate motions that make up a step are referred to individually they are called *botte* (literally "strokes").

The *sonata*, or music which accompanies the dance, is made up of a number of strains. Negri, in his directions to the musicians, refers to these strains, as well as to the dance figures, as *parte*, but it seems best to use a different word in our discussion because the musical strains do not necessarily correspond in length to the dance figures. The music for some balli consists of a single strain that is repeated over and over to accompany five or six dance figures; sometimes a strain must be repeated several times to provide enough music for a single figure. When the music has several strains Negri gives very explicit directions for adapting it to the dance. This often results in a very complex organization. For the balletto *Leggiadra marina*, for instance, the instructions read: "The first two strains are to be played twice each, the gagliarda is played twice, the sciolta twice, then comes a return to the first strain which is played twice, then the gagliarda twice, then the first strain twice again and thus ends the ballo." All this is used to accompany eight dance figures, the third and the sixth of which are inscribed "mutatione della sonata in gagliarda."

Structural organizations of this sort do not conform to any set pattern but vary in the different balli and balletti. The music consists of a certain number of strains, but these may repeat or recur any number of times and in any order; sometimes, indeed, the same "sonata" is used for two or more balli which have different numbers of figures, the repetitions and recurrences of its strains being adjusted to suit the particular dance. It is evident, then, that the only unit that can be used for consistent comparison between dance and music is the single strain. Negri states that in most of the balletti one finds phrases of eight perfect beats of music ("Nella maggior parte dei balletti intervengono otto battute perfette di musica.").[3] If we assume that Negri's eight perfect

3. *Op. cit.*, p. 104.

beats are equivalent to eight tactus or the value of eight semibreves under the normal signature C, we find that this statement is generally borne out by the music. We do encounter, however, strains of six or twelve semibreves, and in many cases the eight tactus strains are composed of four tactus of music repeated. Furthermore, the tactus sometimes falls upon the dotted semibreve or the dotted minim, and the beats below the level of the tactus are subdivided in diverse ways according to the meter of the particular dance.

It becomes apparent that several levels of meter must be taken into account in order to make a consistent comparison between the metric structures of the various dances. Each level of meter obviously arises through the duple or triple division of the note values of the next higher level. It should therefore be possible to determine *all* levels of meter of a given strain of music by following the process of grouping pulses to the point where a single note is divided into two or three equal parts to produce a duple or triple beat. The eight tactus of Negri's "normal" strain together have the value of a single maxima. If we take this value as a starting-point and analyze the various ways in which it is divided and subdivided in different dances we should arrive at a basis for comparing their metric structures, and for discovering, for instance, just how a ballo was converted into a gagliarda or corrente.

The reader will recall that Brunelli begins his elucidation of rhythmic notation with the statement that under the sign of *tempo maggiore imperfetto* the *maxima* is worth eight tactus, the *longa* four, the *breve* two, the *semibreve* one, the *minima* one half, the *semiminima* one fourth, the *croma* one eighth, and the *semicroma* one sixteenth. He is here following a precedent established by theorists of the sixteenth century and even earlier who always included in their treatises paradigms or tables showing the values of the notes under the various mensuration signs for perfect or imperfect modus, tempus, and prolation. There is evidence that these tables were not solely of theoretical importance but were actually used by composers in setting up metric schemes to serve as structural units for their works. Even when no maxima actually appeared in a composition the metric scheme which resulted from its various subdivisions was often used as a basis for the divisions or sections of the total structure.[4]

If, as seems likely, this practice was continued into the seventeenth century, our attempt to analyze the metric levels of these pieces will actually be reversing the procedure used in musical composition. If not, we shall, at any rate, accumulate information that will be useful in comparing the pieces. The vague-

4. Cf. O. Gombosi's transcriptions showing regular organization of *Grosstakt* meters, *Journal of the American Musicological Society*, I, 2 (1948), p. 52 and *Musica Disciplina*, IV (1950), p. 45.

ness of seventeenth-century notation as compared to the precision of the mensural system is bound to be a hampering factor; it will occasionally be necessary to resort to hypotheses, especially in determining the higher levels of meter. The decline of mensural notation must be attributed primarily to the increasing use of the smaller note values and the corresponding disuse of large values. When no more than a single *longa* appeared in a piece (and that usually only as a final note) there was no need to indicate to the performer whether the modus was perfect or imperfect. By the first decade of the seventeenth century breves were rarely used. Pieces which, from a structural point of view, were actually in *tempus perfectum* (𝆸 = 𝆹 𝆹 𝆹) could therefore be written under the imperfect mensuration sign C, the occasional appearance of a perfect breve being designated by a dot of addition. Similarly, the mensuration formerly designated as major prolation (⊙ or Ͼ, 𝅝 = 𝅗𝅥 𝅗𝅥 𝅗𝅥) became identified with *sesquialtera* and was written, using dotted semibreves, under the signature C $\frac{3}{2}$, C3, or simply 3. At the same time the copious use of semiminims and *crome* (eighth notes) introduced two new levels of meter lower than that of prolation.

In analyzing the characteristic metric schemes of these dances, the set of symbols introduced by Willi Apel [5] to designate imperfect and perfect modus, tempus, and prolation will be used and extended to include levels of meter below that of prolation, as follows:

Maxi-modus $\underline{\text{II}}$ and $\underline{\text{III}}$ = relation of longa to maxima

𝆶 = 𝆷 𝆷 𝆶· = 𝆷 𝆷 𝆷

Modus II and III = relation of breve to longa

𝆷 = 𝆸 𝆸 𝆷· = 𝆸 𝆸 𝆸

Tempus 2 and 3 = relation of semibreve to breve

𝆸 = 𝆹 𝆹 𝆸· = 𝆹 𝆹 𝆹

Prolation $\underline{2}$ and $\underline{3}$ = relation of minim to semibreve

𝆹 = 𝆹𝅥 𝆹𝅥 𝆹· = 𝆹𝅥 𝆹𝅥 𝆹𝅥

ii and iii = relation of semiminim to minim

𝆹𝅥 = 𝆹𝅥𝅮 𝆹𝅥𝅮 𝆹𝅥· = 𝆹𝅥𝅮 𝆹𝅥𝅮 𝆹𝅥𝅮

$\underline{\text{ii}}$ and $\underline{\text{iii}}$ = relation of croma to semiminim

𝆹𝅥𝅮 = 𝆹𝅥𝅯 𝆹𝅥𝅯 𝆹𝅥𝅮· = 𝆹𝅥𝅯 𝆹𝅥𝅯 𝆹𝅥𝅯

5. Willi Apel, *The Notation of Polyphonic Music*, p. 17ff.

In the following examples an attempt has been made to reconstruct the total metric schemes of a number of dance strains. As said before this analysis must be partly hypothetical because of the ambiguity of the notation. The chief problems arising from this ambiguity fall into two main categories: (1) the interpretation of the signature 3, which, when it appears with no indication of the *tempo*, may refer to the triple grouping of semibreves, minims, or semiminims; (2) the determination of whether semibreves and minims appearing under the signature C should be grouped by twos or threes. The hypotheses used in constructing these charts have not been adopted without supporting evidence. The most useful clues are those derived from the comparison of different metrical versions of the same tune. In the case of a ballo that is transformed into a gagliarda or a corrente, for instance, it may be assumed that the salient profile of the strain will remain the same; the tones corresponding to the main thetic points of the melody should therefore coincide in the duple-beat and the triple-beat version. The following comments are offered in justification of my solutions to the above-mentioned problems.

Example 33. The figure 3 in the gagliarda to Negri's *La Galeria d'Amore* (Ex. 33b) refers to the triple grouping of minims for the following reasons: semiminims must be grouped by twos because of the preponderance of plain (not dotted) minims in the second half of the tune; the six minims before the first thetic point of the melody (the semibreve g′) are therefore to be interpreted as three groups of two, not two groups of three, and the whole strain consists of four dotted semibreve beats. The proper signature, according to Brunelli, would be , *sesquialtera minore*, and the piece should be performed to an unequal tactus.

EX. 33

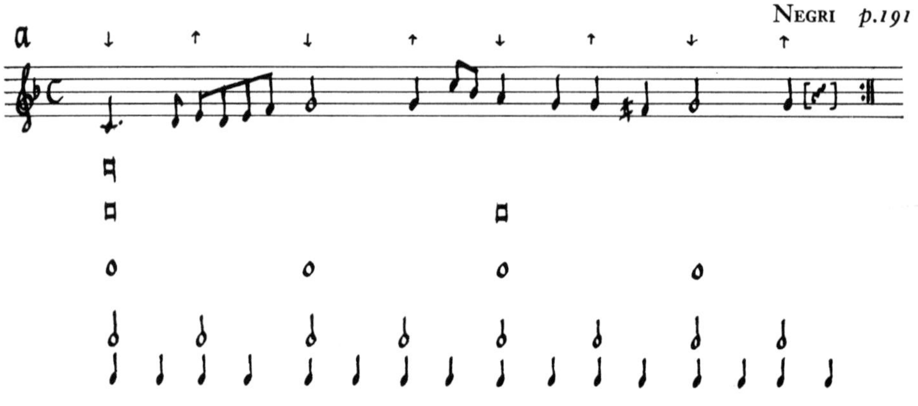

Example 34. The figure 3 in the gagliarda to *Amor Felice* (Ex. 34b) implies a triple grouping on two levels—that of the minim and that of the dotted semibreve. A duple grouping of the minims is ruled out because it would produce continual syncopation. The ballo melody (Ex. 34a) divides into

EX. 34

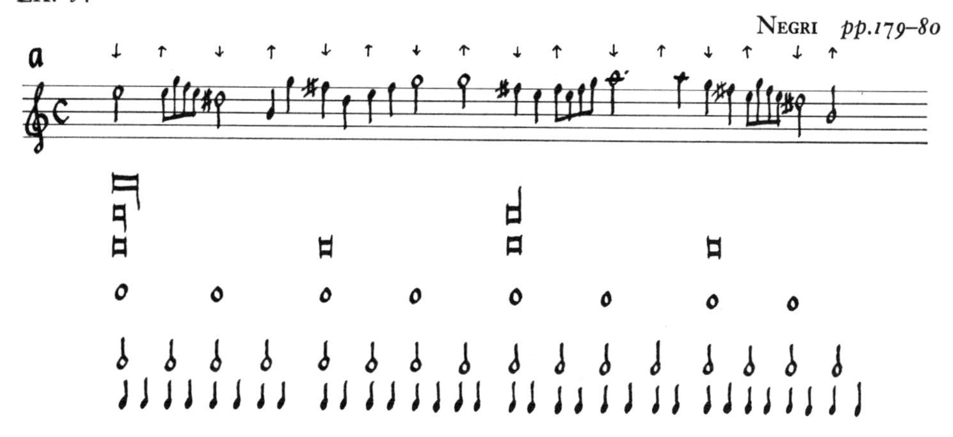

phrase members of two tactus each, beginning on the notes e″, f♯″, f♯″ and g″. These notes in the gagliarda are separated by values equivalent to three dotted semibreves; the dotted semibreves must therefore be grouped in threes in order to bring these salient notes of the melody into corresponding positions in the phrase members.

Gagliarda

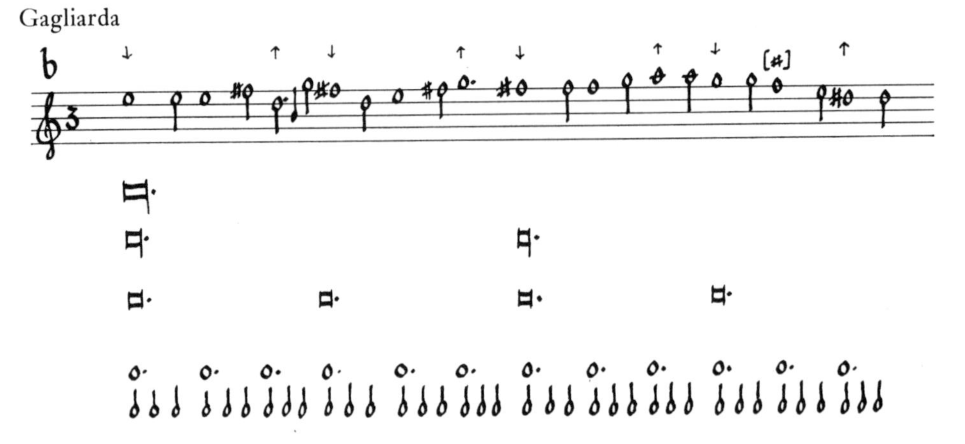

Example 35. The signature C3 in Zanetti's corrente refers to a triple grouping of semiminims, as evidenced by the persistent alternation of minim and semiminim throughout the melody. The sixteen groups of M + SM which make up the strain divide evenly into pairs, so that an even tactus with three SM on the downstroke and three SM on the upstroke is probably intended. The signature C^{6}_{4} would have indicated this meter more precisely.

EX. 35
Corrente

Zanetti *p.133*

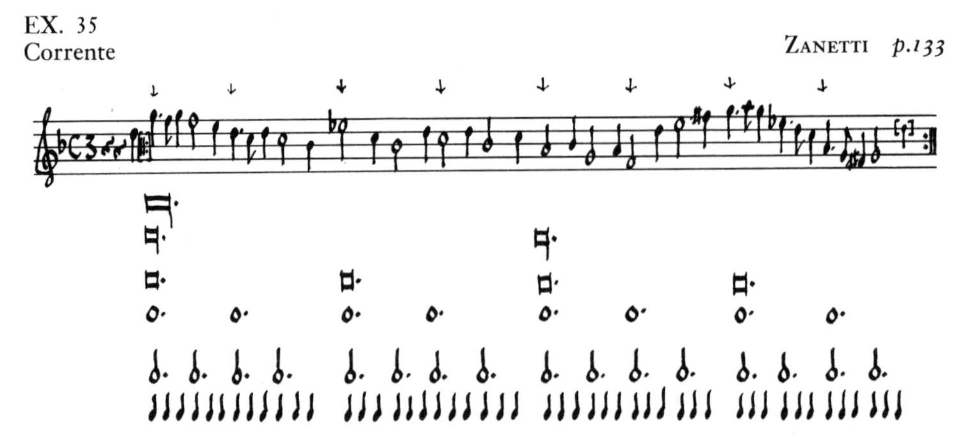

Example 36b. The C3 in Zanetti's corrente version of the ballo entitled *Spagnoletto* (shown in Ex. 36a) implies a triple grouping of minims, due to the

consistent alternation of semibreves and minims. These groups also occur in pairs, so that the resulting meter is the same as that of Example 35 in spite of the fact that larger note values are used.

EXAMPLE 37a. The first strain of Brunelli's *Ballo Grave* clearly divides in the middle; after the two minim d″s the pattern of note values is repeated exactly. This shows that the six-tactus strain is made up of 2 x 3 semibreves, not 3 x 2. This triple grouping of semibreves really implies *tempo perfetto* ⊟ = ◇ ◇ ◇ for which the proper signature is O, but Brunelli rarely employs this sign even though he explains it in some detail in his treatise.

EX. 37

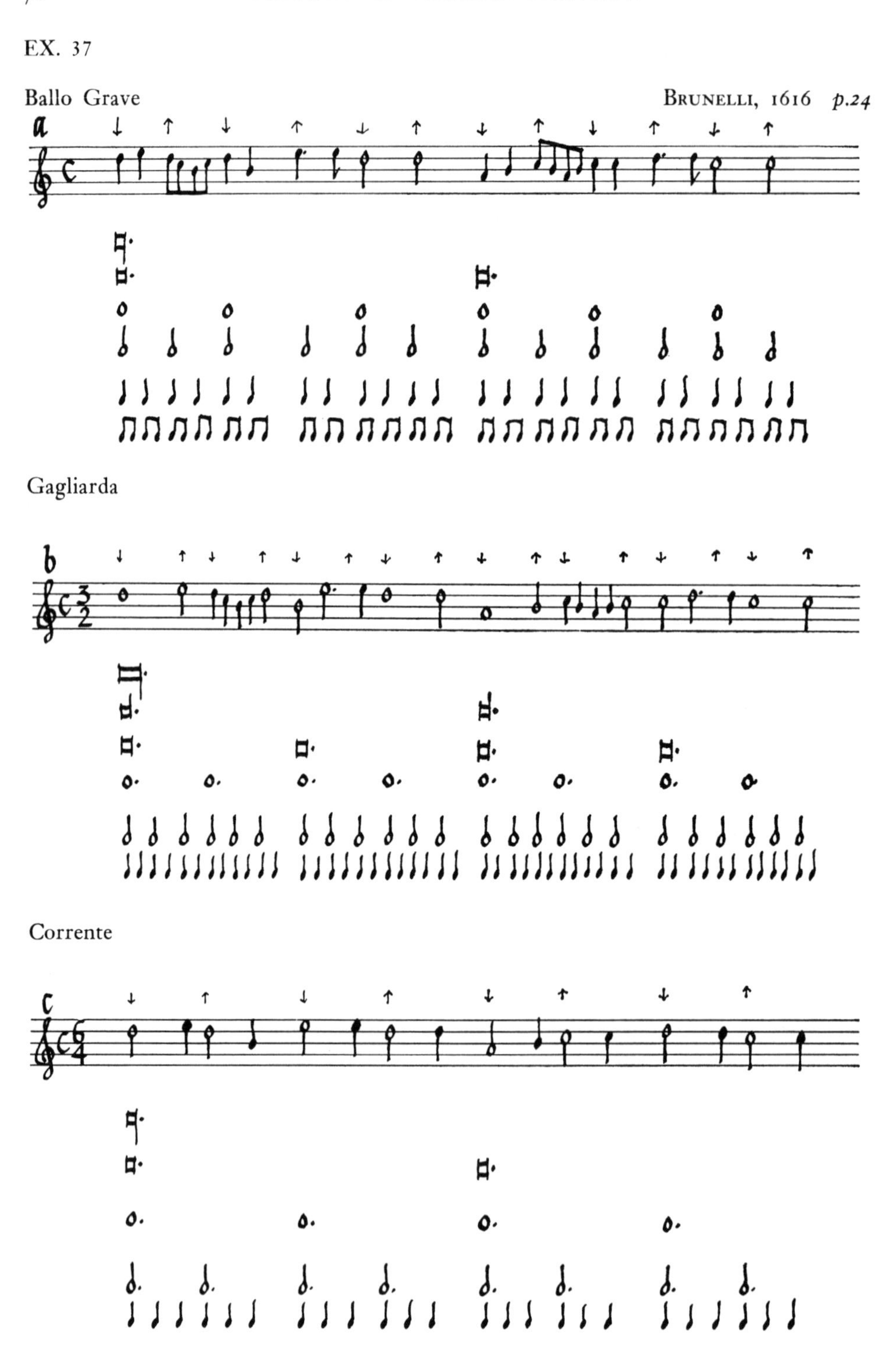

EXAMPLE 38. Negri's *Tordiglione* (Ex. 38a) and Zanetti's almost identical *Tortaglione* (Ex. 38b) are both examples of the dance known in France as the tordion. Their meters are obviously the same though they are notated in different time values and with different signatures. Negri's version illustrates the triple grouping of minims, Zanetti's the triple grouping of semibreves. The strain clearly divides into two phrases of equal length after the minim d′, that is, just before the skip of the octave. Each of these phrases divides into two equal phrase members. The phrase members have the value of a dotted semibreve in Negri's version, a dotted breve in Zanetti's version. Negri's tactus falls on the semibreve and Zanetti's on the breve, so the phrase member in each case consists of 1½ tactus; in other words, half-tactus are grouped in threes.

EX. 38

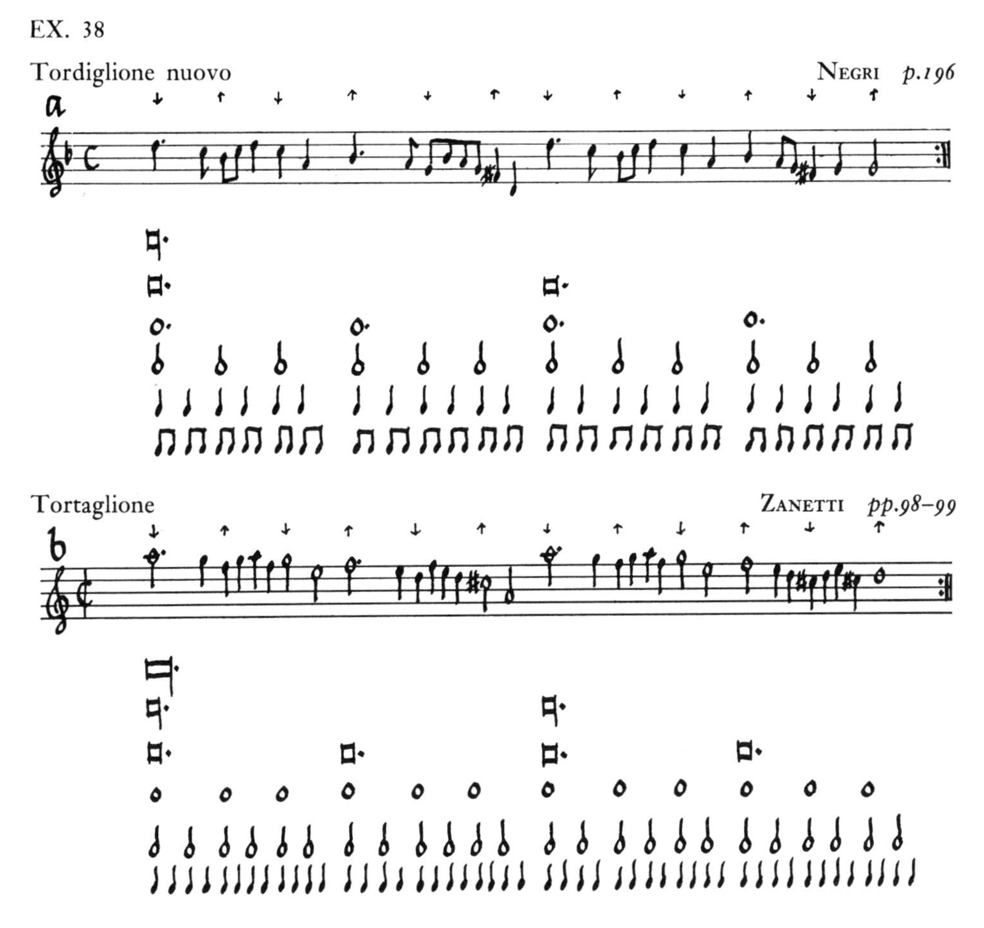

EXAMPLE 39. The figure 3 in the gagliarda to Zanetti's ballo (Ex. 39b), *Speranza d'Amore*, indicates a triple grouping of minims, which are related

to the minims of the ballo in the relation 3:2—i.e. tactus of three minims (gagliarda) = tactus of two minims (ballo). Another triple grouping occurs in both dances at the level of the longa, since the twelve-tactus strain is made up of three groups of four tactus each (Mx = 3L).

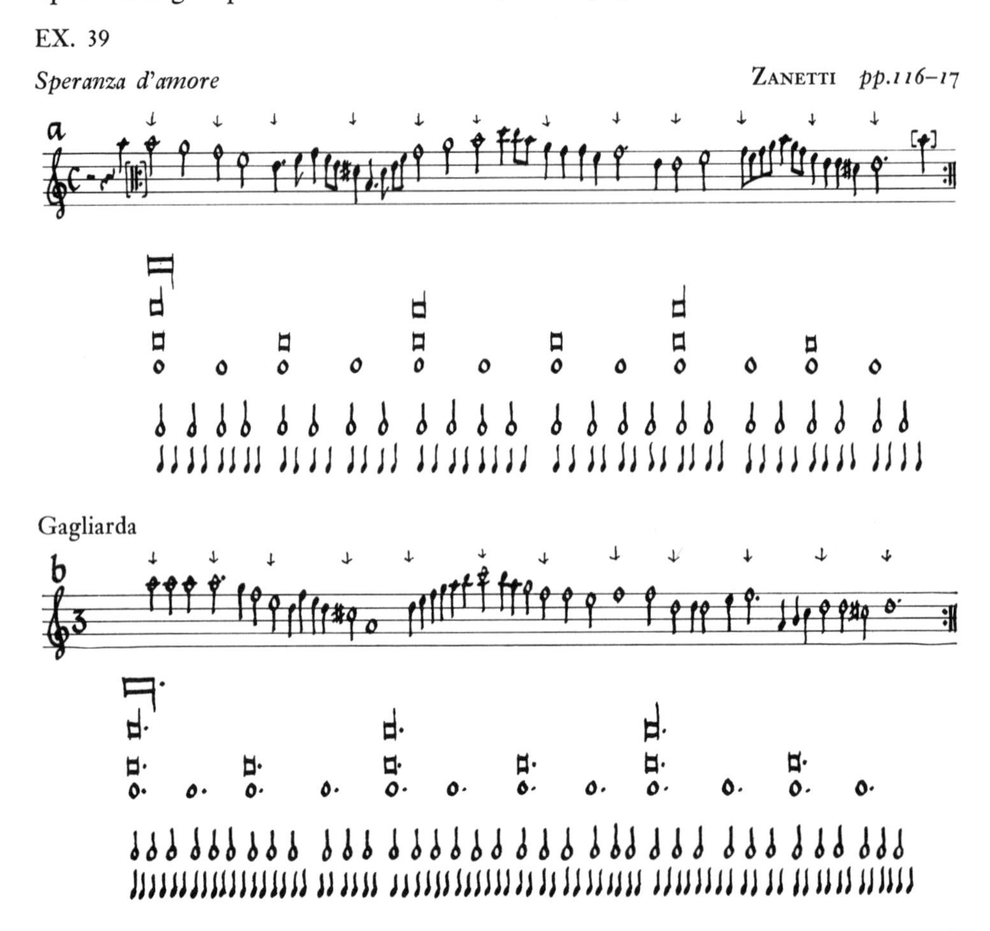

EXAMPLE 40. It is evident from these last examples that the higher levels of meter coincide with those aspects of musical form that are usually called phrase structure or period structure. The *Pas è mezzo* (Ex. 40a) and saltarello (Ex. 40b) by Zanetti illustrate this structural use of meter on a level still higher than any we have discussed thus far. The bass lines of the two dances are juxtaposed in Example 41a and b; the traditional bass of the *passamezzo moderno*, which is used as a skeleton, is shown in Example 41c and d. It will be seen that the eight semibreves of the customary dance strain are here expanded to the value of eight longs in the *Pas è mezzo* and eight dotted breves in

the saltarello. These durations are used to establish points of arrival at which the bass notes of each of the dances coincide with the notes of the skeleton melody. The lower levels of meter result from the division of each of these segments into four even tactus (four semibreves) for the passamezzo and two uneven tactus (two dotted semibreves) for the saltarello.

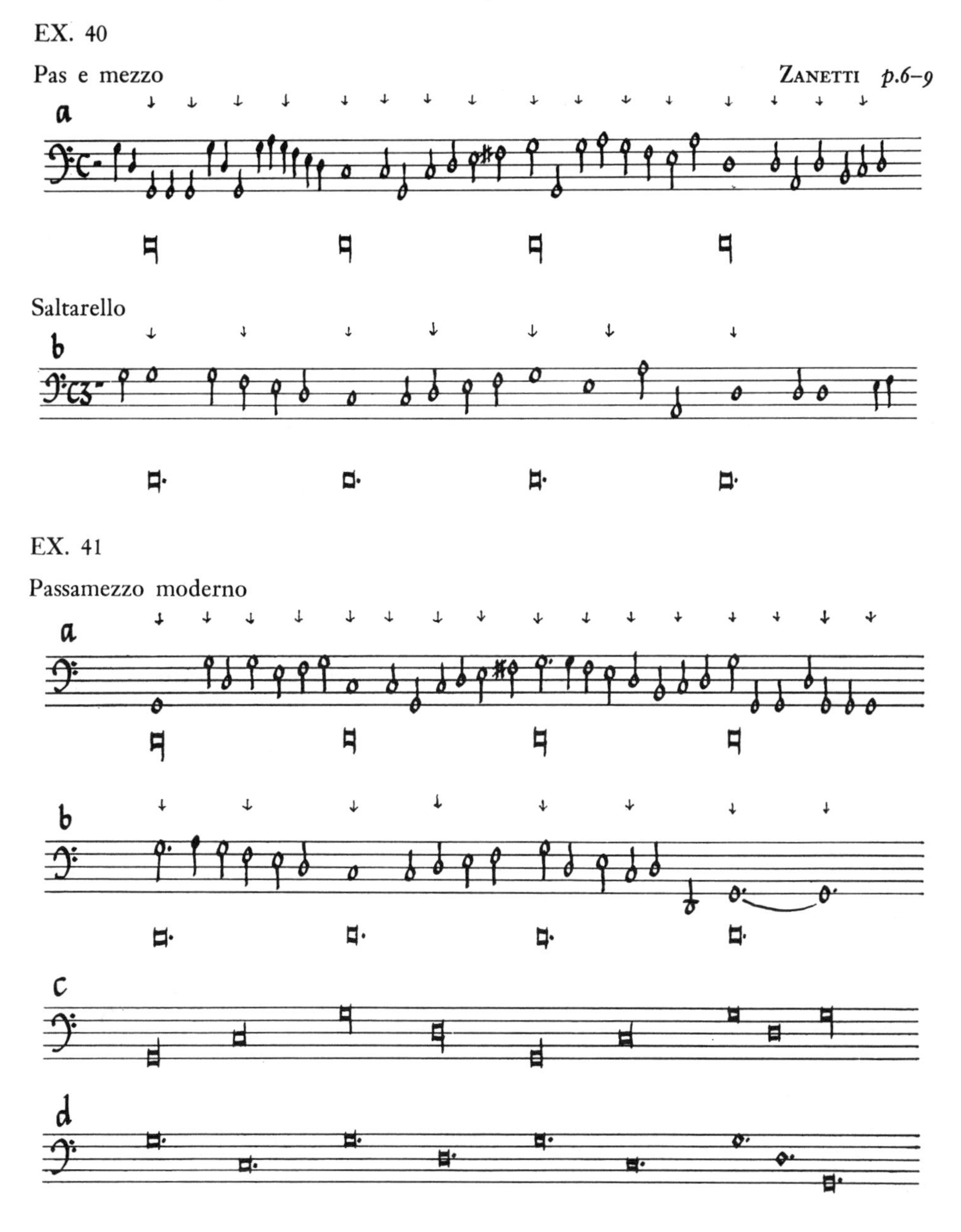

We have seen that the higher levels of meter govern the larger aspects of form in these dance pieces. It is the lower levels, on the other hand, that govern those details of metrical structure that distinguish one type of dance from another. If we review the three lowest levels of all the metrical schemes that have been analyzed in the foregoing charts we can distinguish three main categories: (1) those in which the beats are duple throughout, II, 2, *2* and 2, *2*, ii; (2) those in which a triple beat occurs on some level higher than the lowest, 2, *3*, ii; 3, ii, *ii* and II, 3, *3*; (3) those in which a triple beat occurs only on the lowest level 2, ii, *iii* and 2, *2*, iii. To the first category belong most of the balli; to the second the gagliarda, saltarello, and tordaglione; to the third the corrente and canario.

We observe, moreover, that there are several ways of converting a ballo into a gagliarda, according to the level of meter upon which the beat is changed from duple to triple. If the change is effected on the level of the tactus in both dances the even tactus of the ballo becomes the uneven tactus of the gagliarda, the semibreves of the former being replaced by the dotted semibreves of the latter, as in *La Galeria d'amore* (Ex. 33) and *Speranza d'Amore* (Ex. 39). Assuming that the tempo of the tactus remains approximately the same, the three minims of the gagliarda will be performed in the same time as two minims of the ballo, and the two dances will have the same duration.

The change may also be brought about by equating the tactus of one dance to two tactus of the other. In *Amor Felice* (Ex. 34b), for instance, the dotted breve (tactus) of the gagliarda corresponds to the breve (two tactus) of the ballo. This is actually the same relationship that exists between the saltarello and *Pas è mezzo* of Example 40. The dotted semibreve of the saltarello corresponds to the breve of the *Pas è mezzo*. The equation of note values differs from that of Example 34, but in both cases one tactus of the triple meter corresponds to two of the duple meter.[6]

Brunelli's suite of dances is an exceptional case owing to the unusual ternary

---

6. Thomas Morley apparently considers this to be the normal relationship between pavan and galliard. In his *Plaine and Easie Introduction to Practical Musicke* (p. 181) he writes: "Looke how many fours of semibreves you put in the straine of your pavan, so many times six minims must you put in the straine of your galliard."

That is:

↓ ↑↓ ↑ ↓↓↓↓

𝅗𝅥 𝅗𝅥 𝅗𝅥 𝅗𝅥 𝅗𝅥 𝅗𝅥 = 𝅝 𝅝 𝅝 𝅝

In Italy, however, we find that although this is the most common passamezzo-saltarello relationship it is less frequent between ballo and gagliarda than is the one-to-one relationship of Example 33.

structure of the *Ballo Grave* (Ex. 37a). The triple grouping of the semibreves in the ballo is equated with the duple grouping of the dotted breves of the gagliarda, which is still one level above that of the tactus. This brings about a ratio of 4:3 between the tactus of the two dances.

The conversion of a ballo into a corrente or a canario is usually effected simply by changing the lowest level of meter from duple to triple, adding, repeating, or omitting notes as necessary to make the tactus coincide. It is important to note, however, that this lowest level is not necessarily represented by the same time values in the two versions. In the spagnoletto (Ex. 36), for instance, the minim beat (½ tactus) of the ballo corresponds to the dotted semibreve (½ tactus) of the corrente. The Brunelli pieces are again exceptional. The transformation takes place on the level of the dotted breve in both dances but owing to the difference in mensuration (ballo C, corrente C^{6}_{4}) two tactus of the corrente complete the same portion of the melody as three tactus of the ballo, so the relationship is 3:2.

Rhythmic Patterns in Music and Dance

THE TIME during which a piece of music takes place is organized in a hierarchy of durations corresponding to the various time values that are shown in the foregoing tables of metrical schemes. These are grouped in such a way that each duration may be regarded as a subdivision of the next longer duration. Speaking in terms of meter this means that each of the subdivisions, and the musical tone or tones contained in it, may be construed as an arsic or thetic pulse (as the case may be) of a beat on the next higher level. The thetic pulse of each beat has the quality of a point of arrival in relation to the preceding arsic pulse. Similarly, when the beats are grouped in measures, the thetic beat of each measure has the quality of a point of arrival from the preceding arsic beat. On each level of meter there occurs a continuous alternation of thetic and arsic pulses and beats. In this unbroken succession of arses and theses no articulation is possible until some particular beat arrives which is felt to be more thetic than those which precede it and thus marks a point of repose in the flow of the music. Rhythmic patterns, each of which must have a beginning and an end, and which often have a point of climax somewhere in between, are set off from each other by these points of articulation. There is nothing in the notation, as far as time signatures, barlines, or note values are concerned, that specifically points out the position of these articulations. It is true that other musical factors, such as melodic or harmonic cadences, the repetition or recurrence of melodic configurations or patterns of note values, do provide clues to the whereabouts of these thetic points. Clues such as these have been used in drawing up our charts of total metric schemes. They are, however, neither infallible nor ubiquitous, and since we need all the information we can get in order to establish the nature and identity of rhythmic patterns, the next step will be to investigate certain dance rhythms and their relations to the rhythmic patterns of music.

Dance, like music, occupies time. The time during which a dance takes place is likewise organized in a hierarchy of durations corresponding to the time values in the metrical scheme of a piece of music. These durations, instead of being expressed through musical tones, are made manifest through bodily movements. The movements are grouped into pulses and beats quite analogous to the grouping of their music counterparts. The arsic and thetic qualities of the elements that make up dance patterns are more easily discerned, because they are visible, than they are in musical pulses and beats. The patterns of motion and repose, tension and relaxation, are materialized in physical movements that can actually be seen—the muscles tense and relax, the human body is active or at rest—and the moments at which these events occur may be described as arsic or thetic.

It must be recognized that "arsic" and "thetic" are always relative terms, just as the processes they describe can only be understood as relationships. No event is arsic in an absolute sense, but only more or less arsic than another; there are no completely thetic moments in a dance or a piece of music except the final stop at the end. It is because of this relativity of motion and repose throughout a piece of music or a dance that a consideration of several levels of meter is essential to our analyses. A moment that may be described as thetic on one level of meter will be found to be arsic on a higher level. A thetic beat that marks the end of a rhythmic pattern may be only the midpoint of a larger rhythmic pattern that takes place on a higher level of meter.

Fortunately the seventeenth-century authors of dance treatises recognized the importance of levels of meter. All dance movements and steps are described by them in terms of the number of beats it takes to perform them. Unlike the musical theorists, for whom *battuta* always meant tactus, the dancing masters treated the beat according to its true nature. They distinguished three kinds: the *battuta perfetta*, the *battuta ordinaria*, and the *battuta minima*, corresponding to beats on three different levels of meter, and in stating the duration of a dance movement they specified the kind of beat used as a unit of measurement.

One of the problems of interpreting directions for executing dance movements lies in the difficulty of distinguishing which part of the movement described takes place *before* the beat, which part precisely *on* the beat, and which part *during* the beat. In general it must be assumed that the moment of the dancer's contact with the ground is to be synchronized with the thesis of the beat. This, indeed, was the original significance of the term "thesis" as used by the ancient Greeks. It follows from this assumption that any motion preparatory to the contact with the ground must occur *before* the thesis of the beat, that is, sometime during the preceding arsis. We are therefore obliged to accept the seemingly self-contradictory proposition that very often a movement described as occupying two beats does not coincide with the duration of those two beats but actually begins before the first and comes to an end at the beginning (i.e. the thesis) of the second beat.

This ambiguity is not inherent in the metrical and rhythmical events themselves; it must be blamed on the inadequacy of terminology and musical notation, both ancient and modern. In reality every beat, whether it occurs in music or in dance, begins with an arsis. When a piece or a phrase of music starts without an "up-beat" the arsis to the first beat is not heard, though of course it may be *seen* in the preparatory movement of the dancer or conductor. The first arsis is therefore considered imaginary or non-existent, and the term that should designate it is applied to the second part of the first beat, which really doesn't belong to the first beat at all, being the arsis of the second beat. This throws the whole sequence of events out of its proper order. For example, in a series of four quarter note beats which consists of eight pulses that are alternately arsic and thetic, the arsis of beat 1 is often the *second* arsis of the dance movement, since the first (silent) arsis is neither seen on paper nor heard in the music, but is felt by the musicians and seen in the dancer's or conductor's preparatory movement:

1 2 3 4

(A) T A T A T A T (A)

The equivocation is purely verbal, but it must be taken into consideration in order to avoid confusion. Explanatory comments on this point will therefore be interpolated when necessary in the following analyses of dance movements.

BALLO RHYTHMS

Of the multitude of dance movements used in balli and described by Negri and Caroso only a few of the most characteristic steps can be analyzed here.

The examples are chosen primarily to illustrate the functions of the different levels of meter in determining the lengths and constitutions of rhythmic patterns. Since the present study is not intended to be a dance treatise, Negri's elaborate instructions will be simplified; many of the refinements dealing with the way to hold the body and the exact distances to move toe or heel (measured in "fingers" and "palms") must be omitted. The discussion will be limited to those factors that bear directly upon the correspondence between dance movements and musical rhythm.

In balli that are primarily in duple meter—i.e. those in which the three lowest levels of meter are made up of duple beats—the perfect beat (*battuta perfetta*) usually corresponds to the semibreve, the ordinary beat (*battuta ordinaria*) to the minim, and smallest beat (*battuta minima*) to the semiminim in the original notation; this scale will be maintained here.

Riverenza grave (*.R.*), Slow Honor, occupies four perfect beats. Negri's description runs as follows:

1. On the first beat stand with the weight on the right foot and the left foot advanced a few inches.

2. On the second beat draw the left foot back so that the toe is even with the right heel.

3. On the third beat incline the body and bend the knees.

4. On the fourth beat rise and place the left foot even with the right, lowering the heels.

The following comments are pertinent: (1) If on the first beat we are to stand with the left foot advanced we must have moved it *before* the beat, so that the thesis of the first beat is already a relative point of repose. (2) Similarly, if at the moment of the thesis of the second beat the left foot is to be back even with the right heel it must have been drawn back before the beat, that is during the last part of the first beat. (3) Bowing and bending the knees can very well take place during the third beat, since no contact with the ground is involved, but (4) if on the fourth beat, which is the final of repose, the left foot is to be in position even with right foot, then the rise and movement of the foot must have taken place previously, during the last part of the third beat. In terms of arsis (A) and thesis (T) the pattern may be analyzed thus:

A A A T
→ o o o o
A T A T A A T
1 2 3 4

If we consider the four-beat pattern as a whole the motions that take place on the first three beats must all be regarded as arsic to the point of repose on the thesis of the fourth beat, even though beats one and two are thetic in relation to their preparatory movements on the level of the minim.

Two *Continenze* (.C.), left and right, occupy two perfect beats each. The gentleman takes one step to the left, then joins the right foot to the left. In doing so he must bend his knees, rise to his toes, raising first his left hip (*pavoneggiandosi*), and fall back on his heels. The right .C. is performed in a similar manner.

(1) On the thesis of the first beat the left foot will already have taken its step. The bow, raising of hip, rising to toes, and approaching right foot to left must all take place before (2) the thesis of the second beat, when the feet are together. During the second part of the second beat the right foot makes the preparatory motion for the right .C. Three levels of meter are involved. On the first level the thesis of each beat marks a contact with the ground, therefore a thetic point. On the second level the four-beat pattern divides into two smaller patterns, each .C. having its own point of repose. On the third, still higher level (that of the breve) the first .C. is regarded as arsic to the second.

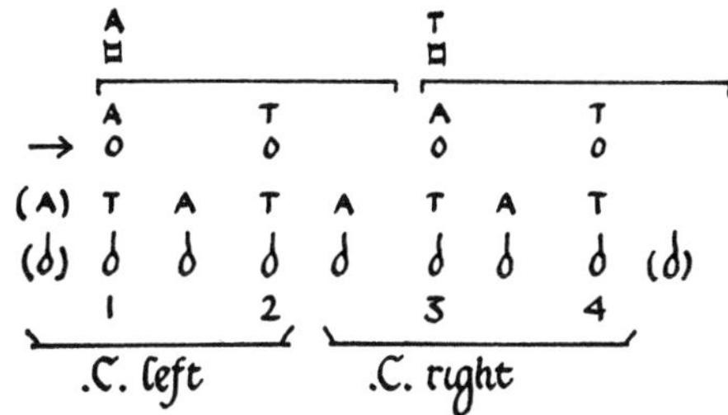

Seguito grave (*.S. grave*), Slow Sequence, consists of three steps performed in the time of four ordinary beats.

1. Step forward on left toe, so that left heel is level with right toe.
2. Step forward on right toe the same distance.

3. Step forward with left foot flat on the ground (*ben in terra spianto*).

4. Stand with both feet flat on the ground.

Although Negri states that one should stand for the whole of the fourth beat without moving (*è vero, che all'ultima battuta, si stà tutto quello spatio di tempo con la persona ferma*), it turns out in practice that it is the *third* beat and the thesis of the fourth that is stationary, as can be seen from the following analysis, which takes account of the arsic movements that precede the first three beats.

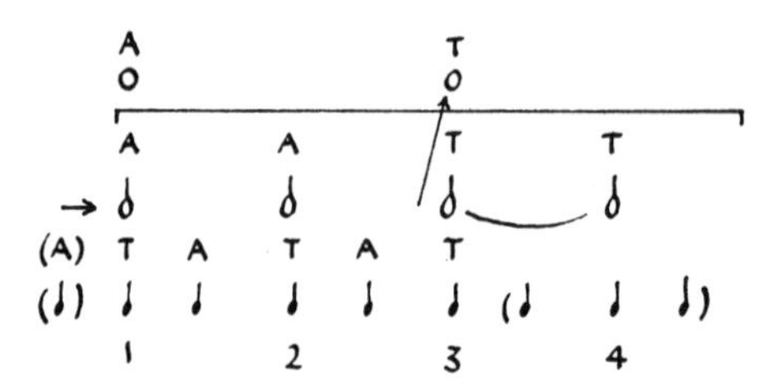

Seguito spezzato (.*SP*.), Broken Sequence, occupies two ordinary beats.

1. Advance the left foot, flat on the ground. Touch the right toe to the ground, rising to toes, and

2. Advance the left foot again, flat on the ground. Then, poise the right foot for the next step.

This step involves only the two lowest levels of meter. In a four-beat pattern composed of two .*SP*., however, the first would be thetic to the second.

A T
(A) T A T A
1 2

The arrows indicate the shift from one level of meter to another. Since the foot touches the ground twice during the first minim the movement actually begins on the level of the semiminim beat, with eighth-note pulses (not shown).

Seguito ordinario (.*S*.), Ordinary Sequence, is a combination of the two preceding .*S*., and occupies four ordinary beats, the first two like the .*S. grave*, the third and fourth like the .*SP*.

1. Step forward on the left toe.
2. Step forward on the right toe.
3. Step forward with the left foot flat on the ground. Touch the right toe to the ground, just behind the left heel, rising to toes, and
4. Step forward flat on the left foot. Then, poise the right foot for the next step.

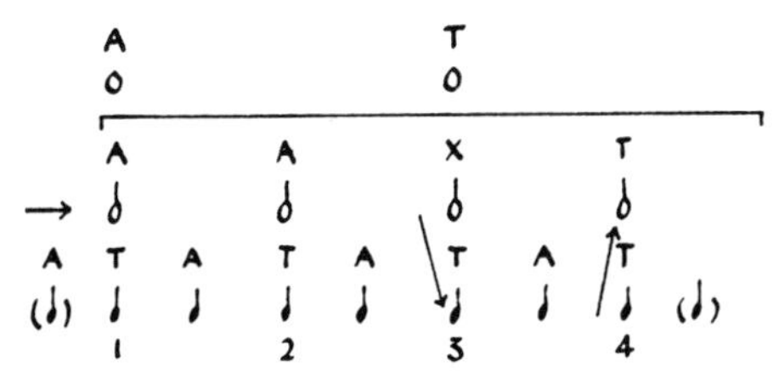

The third beat is particularly ambiguous. Since it comes flat-footed after two steps on the toes it may be construed as a point of repose in relation to them, as in the *.S. grave;* but as the first beat of a *.SP.* it is arsic in relation to the final beat. This double function is the distinguishing characteristic of a *rhythmic climax.* The movement of this pattern can well be described as a rhythmic crescendo toward the third beat and a decrescendo away from it. The rhythmic climax is designated by an X in the analysis.

Fioretto (*.F.*), Flourish, consists of three movements, performed in the time of one ordinary beat or two smallest beats.

Thrust left foot forward in the air, and

1. Jump, landing with the left foot where it was and the right foot a little ahead.
2. Raise left foot, and
3. Hop onto it in the place where the right foot was, at the same time raising the right foot for the next *.F.*

Sottopiede, Underfoot, takes one ordinary beat.

1. Spring sideways to the left, raising the right foot backwards.
2. Thrust the right toe behind the left heel, projecting the left foot forward.

Cadenza, Cadence, is a jump used to close a series of movements. It is performed during the arsis and thesis of one beat, *ordinaria* or *minima*, according to the tempo of the dance.

1. Thrust left foot forward in the air. Jump, drawing the left foot back, and

2. Fall with both feet on the ground, knees bent and the left foot behind the right.

The preparatory forward thrust with the left foot is usually merged with the final thesis of the preceding step, and the jump takes place on the arsis.

T A T (1) 2 T A T (1) 2

Other steps that are performed in the time of one beat are the *Passo presto* (*.P.*), Quick Step; the *Trabuchetto* (*.T.*), Side Leap; and the *Saltino,* Hop.

All the steps described above except the *Riverenza* can begin with either the left or the right foot. The left version has been described in each case since every *series* of dance movements begins with the left foot.

The rhythmic analysis of a complete figure from Negri's *Galeria d'amore* will illustrate the use of some of these step patterns in the structure of a dance form (Ex. 42).

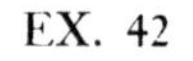
EX. 42

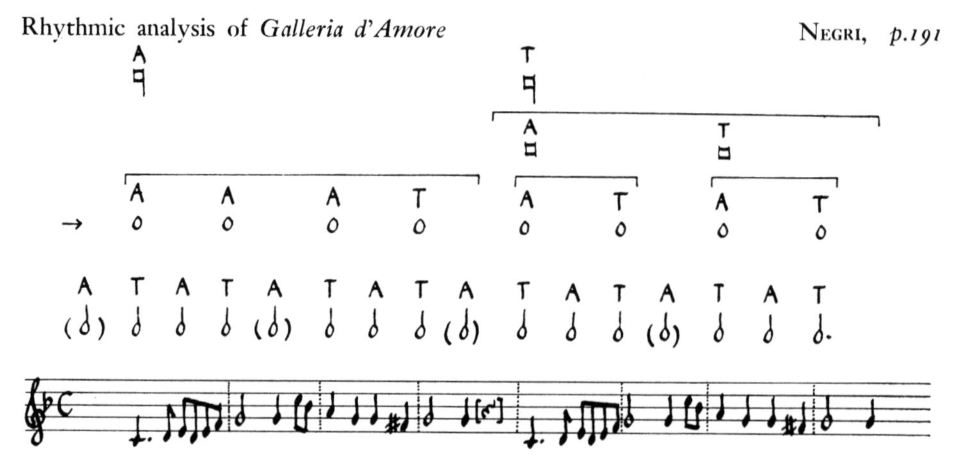

One striking feature of the total form is that it appears to have been constructed on a principle of division similar to that which we have observed in the metric schemes discussed in the previous section. The first strain is divided into two phrases corresponding to the *.R.* and the two *.C.*, each equivalent to the value of a long; the second phrase is again divided into left and right *.C.*, each occupying the duration of a breve. The second strain is also divided into two phrases, each having the value of a long and each containing two *.SP.* and a *.S.*, the first half of each of these phrases being further subdivided into a left and a right *.SP.*

During the first strain the action of the dance takes place on the third level of meter in semibreve beats. In the second strain the body motions become faster, the principal movements being adjusted to the second level of meter in minim beats. This acceleration of motion after the first strain is characteristic of most of the dances described by Negri. They almost invariably begin with a *.R. grave* and two *.C.*, which serve to emphasize the higher levels of metric structure before it is broken up into smaller patterns. The step patterns, indicated by square brackets, all consist of groups of four beats—semibreve beats in the first strain, minim beats in the second. These divisions determine the articulations of the rhythmic patterns and must be observed in the music as well as the dance.

Throughout the first strain a continuous alternation of arsic and thetic minim pulses governs the semibreve beats. In the second strain a continuous alternation of arsic and thetic semiminim pulses provides a metric substructure for the minim beats. Within the groups of four semibreves or four minims, however, the arsic and thetic beats do not alternate regularly. The various distributions of the arsic and thetic beats within these groups are, indeed, the main features that differentiate one rhythmic pattern from another. In this dance we can distinguish four rhythmic patterns, corresponding to the four dance steps:

1. *.R.* Four perfect beats with thesis on the last:

A A A T

2. Two *.C.* Four perfect beats with theses on second and fourth:

A T A T

3. Two *.SP.* Four ordinary beats with thesis on second and fourth:

A T A T

or, combining both levels of meter:

A A T T A T

4. *.S.* Four ordinary beats with climax on third and thesis on fourth:

A A X T

or, combining both levels:

A A X A T

These definitions give the basic characteristics of each rhythmic pattern: Each pattern may be modified to some extent by the degree of emphasis given to the preliminary arsis (upbeat) and by the length of the final thesis.

It must be remembered that these patterns have been derived from the motions of the dance and do not necessarily apply to the music. From the point of view of note values, it seems that the music sometimes actually conflicts with the dance rhythms. At the beginning of the second strain, for example, longer notes occur on the arsic beats of the two *.SP.* than on the thetic beats. The dance, in such cases, produces a sort of rhythmic counterpoint with the music. It is evident from the fact that the steps do not occur in the same sequence in the various figures of the dance which use the same music that the four-beat patterns must be interchangeable. As long as the music provides articulations at the ends of the four-beat groups the step patterns can be adjusted to it in any order. It is quite possible, however, that when percussion instruments were employed they may have used ryhthmic patterns derived from the dance movements, such as T A T T A T from the two *.SP.* and A A T A T from the *.S.* These would add rhythmic emphasis to the accompaniment and they would not necessarily have to coincide with the same steps in the dance.

The balli and balletti cultivated in Italy at the time of Caroso and Negri contained, as we have seen, a vast number of different steps, all classified under distinguishing names. In France the dancing masters followed quite a different system, in which a single pattern with slight variations was repeated throughout a dance, as can be seen in the comparatively simple tablatures published by Thoinot Arbeau in his *Orchésographie*. The interchange and blending of the social arts of France and Italy during the seventeenth century are reflected in the evolution of a type of *ballet de cour* that contains so many elements of both French and Italian origin that it can only properly be described as Franco-Italian. One of the French influences was the tendency to systematize the rhythms of each category of dance—that is, instead of mixing the patterns, as Negri and Caroso do, to keep to a single pattern throughout a dance.[7] It was easy, in these circumstances, for the music to imitate the rhythmic patterns of the dance. Thus we find, in the later dances, that the pattern characteristic of Negri's *.SP.* is used as the prevailing rhythm for the gavotte, and that of the *.S.* for the bourrée in music as well as the dance.

GAGLIARDA RHYTHMS

THE GAGLIARDA, as we have seen, is danced to a meter in which triple beats occur on some level other than the lowest. The next level of meter above that of the triple beats, moreover, is always duple. Three possible notations for this meter, namely *proportione maggiore*, *sesquialtera maggiore*, and *emiolia* have been shown in the dances by L. Allegri quoted in Example 5 of Chapter II. The gagliarda notation used by Negri, however, which is also the one most commonly found in the musical sources, is *sesquialtera minore*, C^3_2, with three minims to the tactus; this scale of note values will be followed in the present discussion. The triple beats, which coincide with the tactus, are written as dotted semibreves, the duple beats on the next higher level as dotted breves and those on the lower level as minims. The presence of dotted notes gives rise to a modification in Negri's terminology for beats. The *battuta perfetta* now refers to the dotted semibreve, the *battuta minima* to the minim. The *battuta ordinaria* is now a beat consisting of two minims or two thirds of a tactus; it can only occur in hemiola. The metric division on the level above

7. Evidence of this tendency is seen as early as 1645 in *Il Dono del Re dell'Alpi* and other balletti produced at the court of Turin by Count Philippe d'Aglié which are preserved in the MS qm II 84 of the Biblioteca Nazionale at Turin. (Cf. also "Le comte d'Aglié et le Ballet de Cour en Italie" by Gino Tani, *Les Fêtes de la Renaissance*, Paris, 1956.) French influence is also apparent in collections of dance pieces published in Italy during the last half of the century, such as Gandini's *Correnti et Balletti alla Francese et all'Italiana*, Venice, 1655.

that of the *battuta perfetta,* consisting of two dotted semibreves or six minims, is called *tempo di gagliarda,* for this is the duration of the *cinque passi,* the basic step pattern of the dance.

Cinque passi (5.*P*.), "five-step," was so named because it contains five steps or movements, performed to six minim beats of music. Negri describes· the simplest form of the 5.*P*. as follows:

> Stand with the weight of the body on the right foot, the left foot advanced a few inches with the toe pointed out a little.
> 1. Hop onto the left foot, raising the right foot forward in the air.
> 2. Lower the right foot and raise the left.
> 3. Lower the left foot and raise the right.
> 4. Lower the right foot and thrust the left foot forward.
> 5. Draw the left foot back and jump,
> 6. landing on both feet with the left foot back, bending the knees.

Steps 5 and 6 constitute the *cadenza delli cinque passi,* which is regarded as a single movement, for on the fifth beat the body is presumably in the air. This accounts for the name, as the movements are counted: right, left, right, left, cadenza. The take-off for the jump of the cadenza is merged with the last forward kick, so the fourth beat fits our definition of rhythmic climax, since it is the point of arrival from the first three kicks and the point of departure for the jump. A rhythmic analysis of the normal 5.*P*., then, would be as follows:

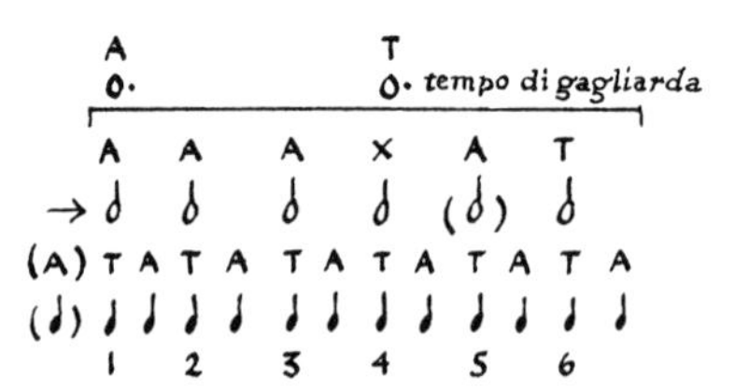

The forward kicks on the first three beats are known as *Passi di gagliarda* (.*P*.), and it is well to note that on a right .*P*. the *left* foot makes the hop touching the ground, and vice versa. While executing the 5.*P*. the dancer may remain stationary, advance, or turn toward the right or left. The step described above is a right 5.*P*.; if it is to be followed by a left 5.*P*. the weight is quickly shifted to the left foot on the arsis of the last beat.

Variants of the simple 5.*P*. include the substitution of side-kicks or back-kicks for the forward .*P*., and of *sottopiede* or plain hops (*saltini*) for the first three .*P*. These variants are all authentic 5.*P*. since, like the basic step, they contain five movements. Other variations, however, increase the number of movements, causing a modification of the rhythmic pattern. If, for instance, two movements are executed during the first beat and the others retain their usual duration the result is a syncopated 5.*P*. (*cinque passi in contratempo*). The first beat may be divided in various ways, the simplest of which is the substitution of a *fioretto in contratempo* for the first step. This variety of syncopated 5.*P*. is described as follows:

Stand with the left foot advanced.

1. Jump, landing with the left foot where it was, the right a little ahead.
2. Hop onto the left foot in the place where the right foot was, at the same time raising the right foot.
3. Lower the right foot, at the same time raising the left backward.
4. Place the left foot behind the right heel and hop onto it, raising the right foot forward.
5. Lower the right foot and raise the left, preparing the
6. Cadenza.

It is not easy to calculate just how the first four movements are to be adjusted to the first three beats of music, but it seems quite certain that the fifth movement, preparing the cadenza, should still come on the fourth beat, so this step would probably produce the following rhythm:

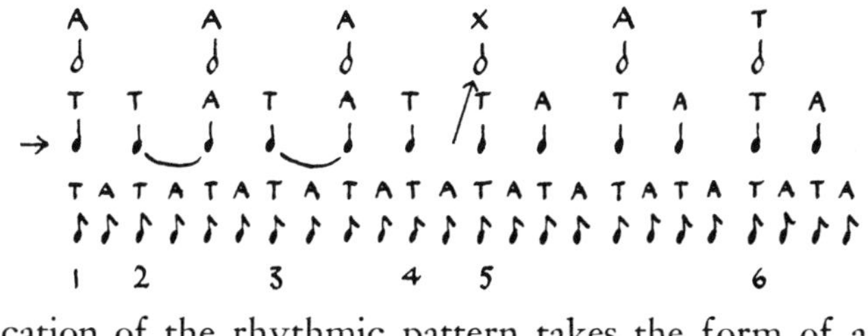

A A A X A T

T T A T A T T A T A T A

T A T A T A T A T A T A T A T A T A T A T A T A

1 2 3 4 5 6

The modification of the rhythmic pattern takes the form of a syncopation (*contratempo*) on the lower level of meter, that of the semiminim. On the upper level the first three minim beats still retain their arsic quality in relation to the rhythmic climax on the fourth.

In other variations of the 5.*P*. the second and third beats or both are broken up into several kicks or hops, leading to a prevailing motion in semiminims throughout the first half of the pattern. Finally, the fifth beat, containing the jump itself, may be broken up by performing various movements in the air

EX. 43

Rhythmic analysis of *Galeria d'Amore* (Gagliarda) NEGRI *p.191*

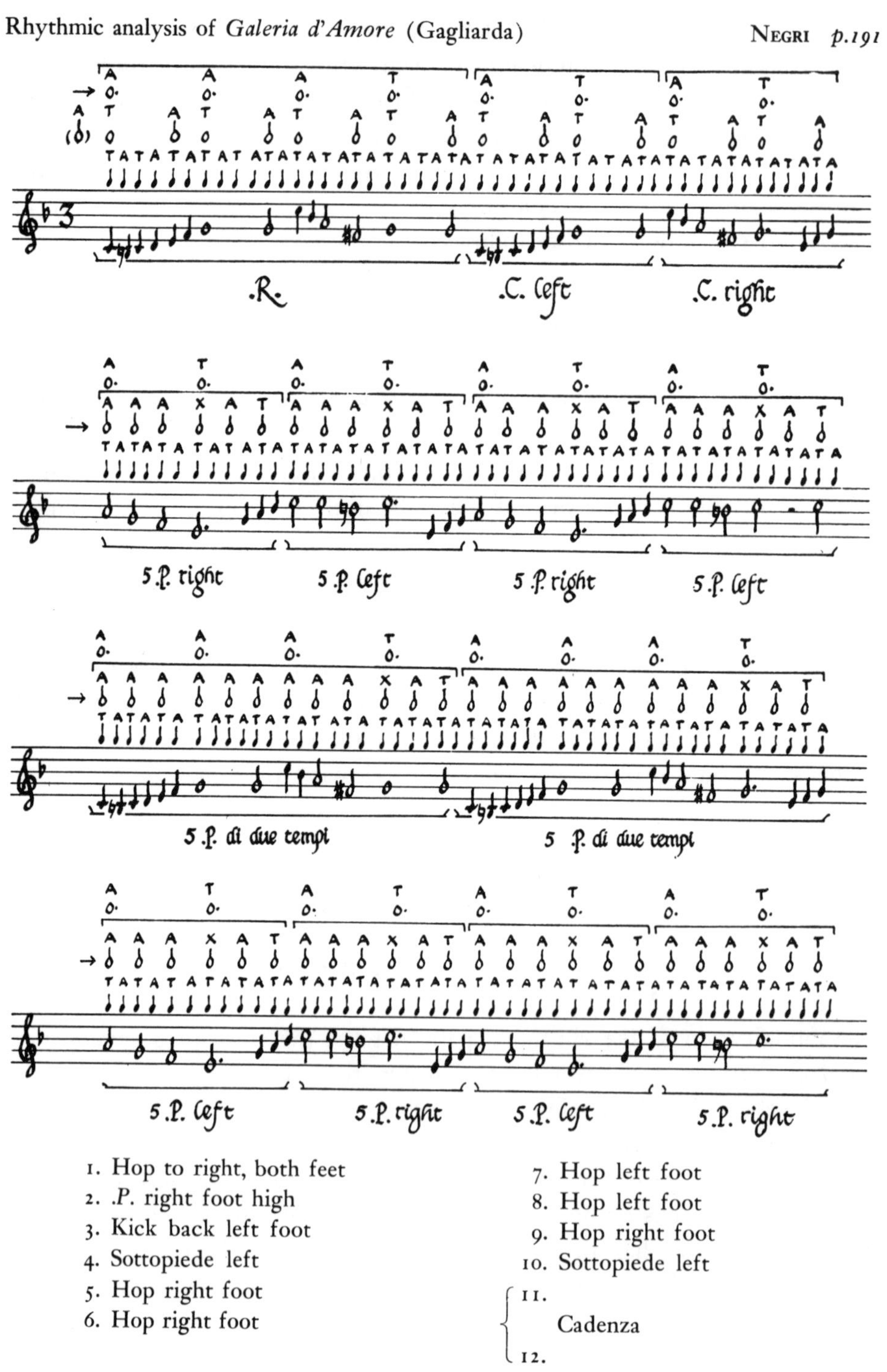

1. Hop to right, both feet
2. *.P.* right foot high
3. Kick back left foot
4. Sottopiede left
5. Hop right foot
6. Hop right foot
7. Hop left foot
8. Hop left foot
9. Hop right foot
10. Sottopiede left
11. } Cadenza
12. }

with the feet and legs. This is the so-called *capriuolo*, or caper. None of these "diminutions," however, influence the basic rhythm of the pattern except in so far as they throw a greater emphasis onto the lower level of meter.

In addition to being varied, the 5.*P*. may be extended by postponing the cadenza from the fifth beat to the eleventh. This extended 5.*P*. is called the *cinque passi di due tempi di gagliarda*, though strictly speaking it is no longer a five-step but an eleven-step, since an extra .*P*. is substituted for the jump on the fifth beat. The first nine beats must all be regarded as arsic to the rhythmic climax on the tenth beat.

Example 43 shows a rhythmic analysis of a gagliarda from Negri's balletto, *Galeria d'amore*. The gagliarda constitutes a single figure of the balletto; it is preceded by a ballo with three figures (one of which has been analyzed in Example 42) and is followed by a canario which completes the balletto with two more figures.

Each of the numbered dance movements is performed to a minim of the Example, so that the 12 movements take up the time of two *cinque passi*. The two strains are each played twice. After the .*R*. and the two .*C*. partners take right arms to dance the two 5.*P*. to the right, then take left arms for the two 5.*P*. to the left. At the recurrence of the first strain partners drop arms and execute the two 5.*P*. *di due tempi* face to face. This section of the dance is known as the *mutanza* (variation). When the second strain recurs the dancers repeat the four 5.*P*. but instead of taking arms they change places twice.

It will be seen that the gagliarda, like the ballo, starts on a higher level of meter than the rest of the dance, the movements of the .*R*. and the two .*C*. being performed to dotted semibreve beats. It is noteworthy that on this level the preparatory movement to each thesis is made on the third minim of the beat, so that thesis and arsis coincide with the downstrokes and upstrokes of the *tactus inaequalis*.

Galeria d'amore is a comparatively simple gagliarda. In more elaborate dances much more complex series of movements are introduced and much use is made of the possibilities of dividing the 5.*P*. into varied numbers of *botte*. The standard unit of measurement for the variations are two, three, or four *tempi di gagliarda*. After his enumeration of the successive steps of a variation Negri always counts up the number of actual body motions the dancers should have made, adding a phrase like "Questa mutanza è di botte 21 in due tempi di gagliarda."

The basic rhythm of the gagliarda may be defined as follows: A pattern in which two levels of meter are clearly perceptible, the higher level consisting of two triple beats with the thesis on the second, the lower level consisting of six duple beats with a rhythmic climax on the fourth followed by an arsis and a thesis on the fifth and sixth.

In seventeenth-century notation the triple beats are accommodated to the *tactus inaequalis* (↓ ↑ ↓ ↑), which explains why Thomas Morley describes the galliard rhythm as being in a trochaic meter.[8] In modern notation the gagliarda rhythm, which has never ceased to be popular and is found in all sorts of musical compositions, is usually written in $\frac{3}{4}$ time. In *God Save the Queen*, for instance, which contains three *tempi di gagliarda* in the first strain and four in the second, each gagliarda pattern occupies two measures. This notation shows neither the grouping of triple beats by twos nor the rhythmic emphasis required on the fourth duple beat. Obviously a compound meter such as $\frac{6}{4}$ or $\frac{6}{8}$ would be more explicit provided the pattern is arranged so that the rhythmic climax falls at the beginning of a measure:

The tempo of the gagliarda could not have been very fast; the leaps themselves demand a certain amount of time, to say nothing of the frequent subdivisions and syncopations on the lower level of meter. A $\frac{6}{4}$ signature therefore seems more appropriate to the dance than does $\frac{6}{8}$, which suggests (though of course it does not prescribe) a more rapid movement.

The music of the gagliarda very often reflects the rhythm of the dance steps, not only in the metric structure but in the arsic and thetic quality of the beats within the pattern. The rhythmic climax on the fourth beat is usually emphasized in the music by means of a longer note—preferably a dotted note, as in *God Save the Queen*. When this does not occur the musical phrase may often be construed as a reflection of the extended 5.*P*. Although this step may be executed to two juxtaposed 5.*P*. patterns, as it was in *La Galeria d'amore*, the music is sometimes adjusted to it by the omission of the rhythmic climax on the fourth beat and the extension of the pattern to twelve beats. The clue to this construction is the treatment of the eighth beat, which, if it is thetic instead of arsic, creates a hemiola—i.e. a $\frac{3}{2}$ measure—in the central portion of the extended pattern. The two patterns may be contrasted as follows:

---

8. "After every pavan we usually set a galliard (that is, a kind of musicke made out of the other) causing it to go by a measure, which the learned call *trochaieam rationem*, consisting of a long and short stroke successivelie, for as the foote trochaeus consisteth of one sillable of two times, and another of one time, so is the first of these two strokes double to the latter; the first being in time of a semibrefe, and the latter of a minime." (*Plaine and Easie Introduction*, p. 181).

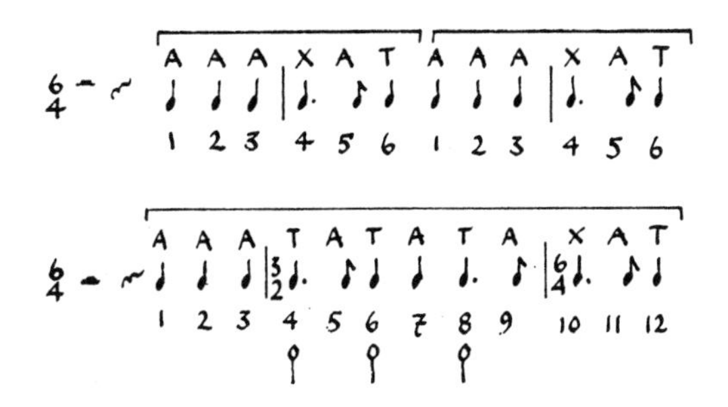

An example of the hemiola pattern may be seen in Brunelli's gagliarda, Examples 16 to 20 of Chapter III, where it is given in both the original notation and in transcription. One advantage of the $\frac{6}{4}$ notation lies in the fact that the hemiola is contained within a single measure, so that it can be interpreted either way. There is no doubt that the music was sometimes purposely ambiguous in order to suit either type of dance step.

The gagliarda to Negri's *Amor Felice* (Ex. 44) presents a special problem to the transcriber because it contains an extra low level of triple beats, the *battuta minima* being represented in this case by the dotted semibreve. Modern notation cannot easily be made to specify three levels of meter. Three possibilities present themselves, none of which is entirely satisfactory: (1) $\frac{6}{4}$ meter with triplets throughout on the lower level, (2) an unusual time signature such as $\frac{18}{8}$ or $\frac{18}{16}$, and (3) $\frac{9}{8}$. The third, being the least cumbersome and the most familiar to the modern reader, is probably to be preferred, although it is the least explicit since it does not indicate the grouping of measures by twos. (See Ex. 44.)

Related dances which employ the rhythmic pattern of the gagliarda are the saltarello, the voltada, and the tordiglione. The saltarello is by far the oldest of all these dances; musical examples dating from the fourteenth century are extant. During the fifteenth century the saltarello was associated with the bassadanza. In the sixteenth and seventeenth centuries it occurs most often as an after-dance to the passamezzo, as in Example 40. The saltarello is not mentioned by Negri; Caroso includes it as a single figure in his balletti *Laura Suave* and *Cortesia,* but does not distinguish its steps from those of the gagliarda. When used as an after-dance to the passamezzo antico or the passamezzo moderno the stability established by the ground bass provides the composer or performer with an opportunity to indulge in a display of melodic and rhythmic virtuosity without obliterating the basic framework. Even in Giovanni Picchi's extravagant saltarello variations for keyboard one can discern the basic gagliarda patterns through a maze of syncopation and hemiola. The less elaborate *Saltarello detto il Lomazzo* by Zanetti is given in the original notation (Ex. 45a) and in a transcription (Ex. 45b) wherein the gagliarda rhythms are indicated by square brackets. Syncopation on the lower level occurs in the second bar, hemiola in the fourth; the last three bars extend the basic six-beat pattern to eighteen beats.

EX. 45

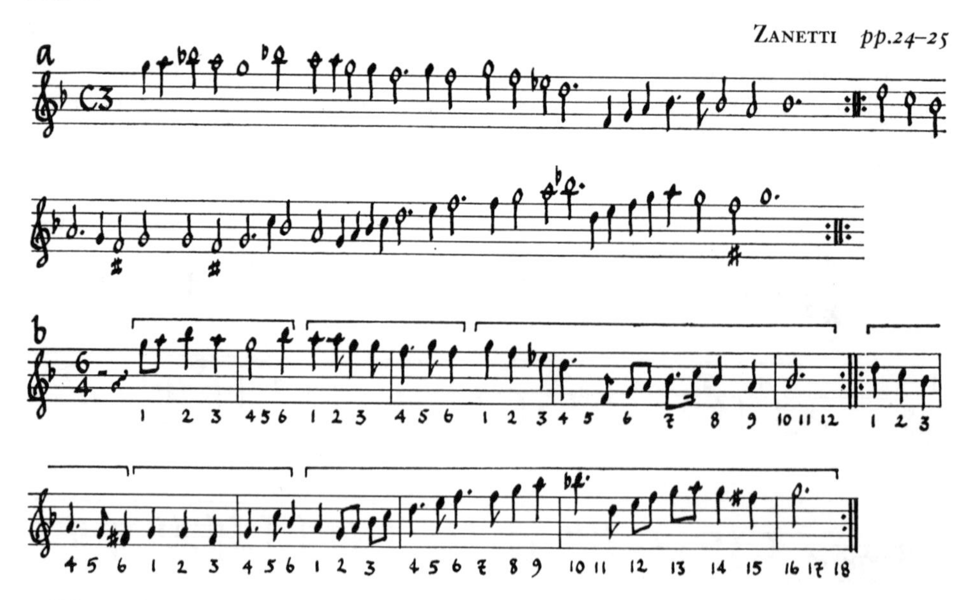

The voltada, which corresponds to the French volta, is the only court dance of the period executed by couples in close embrace. Its rhythm is indistinguishable from that of the gagliarda except that it should probably be taken at a slower tempo to allow for the constant turns which the partners must make together.

An even slower tempo is indicated for the tordiglione by its exceptional notation as well as by its steps, which include a *passo adagio* and a *seguito grave a tordiglione* in addition to the customary gagliarda movements. Negri and Caroso write their tordiglione with the signature C; Zanetti uses the alla breve ¢, but this makes no difference in rhythm or tempo since he doubles the note values. (See Ex. 38.) The notation, in either case, shows that the tordiglione is to be performed to a even tactus, as opposed to the *tactus inaequalis* that regulates other dances in this category. The slow triple beats of the tordiglione occupy three half-tactus each instead of one uneven tactus, as shown in transcription in Example 46.

EX. 46

Tordiglione (see Ex.38a) NEGRI *p.196*

The notation of the tordiglione should serve as a hint that it would be well to watch out for gagliarda rhythms in music that at first sight does not appear to contain triple beats. In the early seventeenth century the rhythm of the gagliarda was in the air; it was played or sung in many different tempos, and when not expressly intended for dancing it was not necessarily regulated by the *tactus inaequalis*. The Sinfonia to Monteverdi's *Incoronazione di Poppea* (Ex. 47a) is a case in point. Here the composer's intention was presumably to call the spectators to attention and at the same time to evoke the pomp and splendor of Nero's court, where the action was to take place. The gagliarda rhythm is slowed down and dragged out into a sustained fanfare. Yet the pattern is clearly recognizable if one disregards the misleading time signature and barlines. The piece consists of eight *tempi di gagliarda*. The rhythmic climax of each pattern is stressed by the characteristic dotted note on the fourth beat. The patterns alternate between six beats and eight. The eight-beat measures do not, however, represent 4 + 4 beats but 5 + 3, so they must be divided into a measure of $\frac{5}{4}$ plus a measure of $\frac{3}{4}$ meter, as shown in the transcription, Example 47b.

EX. 47

Sinfonia MONTEVERDI

CORRENTE RHYTHMS

THE CORRENTE is a rapid dance performed with little hops between most of the steps. The main interest is apparently centered on the movement of the dancers around the room and the changing of partners rather than on the patterns of the individual steps. Negri advises the gentleman to lay aside his cape and his sword in order to dance more gracefully. After the preliminary *Riverenza* the partners dance around with light steps and hops for as long as it pleases them. Then another gentleman will "cut in," and as he does so the first gentleman will make his *Riverenza* and return to his place, whereupon another lady will invite him to dance. This procedure continues until the musicians stop playing.

The steps of the corrente are similar to those of the ballo, but fewer are used and they are less varied. An entire dance may be performed without using more than two different steps, the individual motions of which are always grouped in such a way that they occupy four beats. The steps of the ballo are modified for the corrente by interspersing hops between them. It is quite evident, though not stated in so many words, that the hops are of the hop-step rather than the step-hop variety; that is to say, they are little upbeat hops that serve to propel the dancer from one step to the next in the same way that the hops of the gagliarda are used to project the opposite foot into the air. The natural temporal position for such a hop is the moment immediately before the beat upon which the step is to fall. The short final pulse of a triple beat more nearly approximates this moment than does the pulse of a duple beat. Triple beats in the music therefore provide a more suitable accompaniment for dances that contain many hops than do duple beats. This is probably the reason why most corrente pieces have triple beats on the lowest level of meter.

On the other hand the actual duration of the "upbeat hop" is probably irrational; it takes place a moment before the beat, but no one can say what precise fraction of the beat it occupies. It does not necessarily coincide exactly with the third pulse of a triple beat, and it is quite possible for the dancer to adjust it so that it falls between the two even pulses of a duple beat. Consequently there is no obligation for the composer or the musical performer to maintain triple beats, and this freedom can lead to some interesting rhythmic variety on the lower level in spite of the regularity of the four-beat groups.

According to Negri [9] the ordinary *Seguito* of the ballo becomes a *.S. ordinario con saltino* for the corrente. Its succession of hops and steps may be reconstructed as follows:

Stand with the left foot forward.
1. Hop on the right foot.
2. Step forward on the left toe.
3. Hop on the left foot.
4. Step forward on the right toe.
5. Hop on the right foot.
6. Advance the left foot forward, flat.
7. Touch the ground with the right foot.
8. Step forward flat on the left foot.

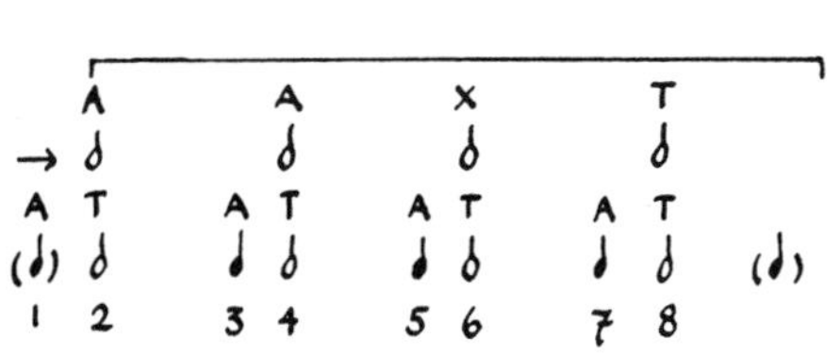

A A X T
→ 𝅗𝅥 𝅗𝅥 𝅗𝅥 𝅗𝅥
A T A T A T A T
(♩) 𝅗𝅥 ♩ 𝅗𝅥 ♩ 𝅗𝅥 ♩ 𝅗𝅥 (♩)
1 2 3 4 5 6 7 8

The rhythmic pattern of the steps is the same as that of the ordinary *.S.*, though the notation will show us that it moves at a faster tempo. In the

9. *Op. cit.*, p. 265.

seguito de quattro .P. in fuga con saltino a *Cadenza* is inserted between the third and fourth beats. This does not alter the pattern except to emphasize still more the rhythmic climax on the third beat, which becomes the take-off for the *Cadenza.* Note that in neither of these steps does a hop precede the fourth beat; the alternation of steps and hops is not necessarily continuous throughout the dance. In place of four-beat patterns like the *.S.* the dancers sometimes execute four *Sottopiedi* or four *Trabuchetti.* In this case the partners turn to the left for one pair of steps and to the right for the other, or vice versa *aggirando intorno da una parte e dall'altra.*[10] The change of direction causes an alteration of the rhythmic pattern A T A T, with a stronger thesis on the fourth beat than on the second. When this sequence is immediately followed by a step of the *.S.* type, the thetic quality of the last one-beat step is attenuated and merges with the *.S.* forming an eight-beat pattern: A T A T A A X T.

If the music furnishes a slight articulation after every four, or at least after every eight beats, any one of these step patterns can be adjusted to it; we find that most corrente melodies favor one or another of these types. In some corrente the melodic or harmonic cadences point to a definite thesis or rhythmic climax on the third beat of each pattern (Ex. 48), whereas in others the the thesis falls consistently on the fourth beat (Ex. 49), and in still others the position of the thesis is not clearly established until the end of the second quatrain, when a thesis on beat 7 (Ex. 50) finally establishes the pattern as A A X T A A T T.

The Florentine composers Calestani (Ex. 48), Brunelli (Ex. 49), and Allegri (Ex. 50) use a notation C^{6}_{4} that clearly indicates the triple beats of the corrente as occupying one half tactus each. Since the A T A T pattern demands a thesis on the second and fourth beats the thesis, in this notation, inevitably falls on the upstroke of the tactus. The modern notation should indicate the arsic beginning by means of rests. A $\frac{12}{8}$ meter is probably the most appropriate for both patterns. The barline should precede the fourth beat in the A T A T pattern (Exx. 48b and d) to show that the last beat is the more thetic. In the A A X T pattern, however, the barline should precede the rhythmic climax on the third beat (Exx. 47b and 49b).

10. *Loc. cit.*

EXAMPLES OF CORRENTE RHYTHMS

EX. 50
Corrente
ALLEGRI p.17
a
b
A A X T A A X T
1 2 3 4 1 2 3 (4)
EX. 51
Corrente
ZANETTI p.133
a
b
A A X T A A X T
A A X T A A X T
EX. 52
Summary of Corrente rhythms
(a) Exx.48a, 49a; (b) Exx.48c, 49c; (c) Ex.48c; (d) Ex.48c; (e) Ex.51a
a b c d e
EX. 53
ZANETTI p.96
a
b
A A X T A A X T A A X T A A X T

EX. 54

NEGRI *p.149*

EX. 55

Corrente

NEGRI *p.204*

EX. 56

Corrente

ZANETTI *p.214*

EX. 57

Corrente

MAGL. XIX, 115 *fol.7*

We shall now turn our attention to the lower metrical levels of the corrente rhythm. Example 52 summarizes the divisions of triple beats that occur in Examples 48 to 50. It is evident that rhythm (a), as it occurs in the simple vocal pieces by Calestani (Ex. 48) and Brunelli (Ex. 49), is the normal basic pattern of the corrente beat, and that all the others are nothing but ornamentations of it. Examples 48c and 49c are, in fact, instrumental variations by Calestani and Brunelli on the song tunes shown in Examples 48a and 49a. The highly elaborate ornamentation in Zanetti's corrente (Ex. 51) is more apparent in the transcription with reduced note values (Ex. 51b) than in the original notation because of the beams that connect the notes that belong to a single beat.

A still more interesting type of rhythmic variation occurs when duple beats are interspersed among the triple beats of the corrente. Let us begin by examining two versions of *Il Cesarino*, one by Zanetti (Ex. 53) the other by Negri (Ex. 54). Zanetti's signature C3 evidently refers to the grouping of minims by threes into dotted semibreve beats. The triple beats are maintained throughout and the patterns, with rhythmic climax on the third beat, fall conveniently into modern $\frac{12}{8}$ meter (Ex. 53b). Negri, on the other hand, uses the *meliola* notation to indicate groups of three semiminims, the 3 being placed between the first and second notes of each group. The 3 in the signature appears to be redundant or erroneous since all of the beats are duple except those specified by the *meliola* sign. The most convenient means of indicating these varied beats in modern notation seems to be $\frac{2}{4}$ with triplets, as in the transcription (Ex. 54b). If this were an isolated case one might suppose that Negri's notation was at fault, and that he intended triple beats throughout as in Zanetti's version. However, the sources contain numerous examples of mixed beats which, though the notation is often equivocal, can usually be fitted nicely into the corrente pattern.

Negri's corrente to the *Bassa Imperiale* (Ex. 55) is a case in point. No *meliola* signs appear, but the 3 in the signature is a warning that triple beats are to be used at appropriate places. The appropriate places turn out to be identical with those for which the author used *meliola* signs in *Il Cesarino*, that is, the characteristic corrente figure ♩. ♪ ♩ (see transcription, Ex. 55b).

The "suggestive" use of the figure 3 is carried still further by Zanetti in his corrente to the *Caccia Amorosa* (Ex. 56). This is obviously a case of "double emploi," in which the performers are expected to collaborate in the creation of the music. The note values, as they stand, cannot be forced into any plausible triple meter. The piece can, of course, be played in duple meter.

EX. 58

Canario
Caroso, 1581 p.181
a
Canario
Zanetti p.102
b
Canario
Negri p.200
c

Triple beats, however, are more suitable for the dance, and Zanetti, by his signature, hints that the performers may introduce them *ad libitum* by altering the unessential note values (i.e. the values of those notes which do not occur on the thesis of a beat) to fit any of the characteristic patterns associated with the corrente. This would result in a performance that would sound something like the transcription shown in Example 56b.

One further variation of the corrente pattern is a hemiola rhythm that occasionally replaces the third and fourth beats. Example 57, from an anonymous manuscript keyboard tablature (Magl. XIX, 115) seems to be another variant of *Il Cesarino*. The hemiola occurs in places that correspond to Negri's insertion of duple beats in Example 54. These are thetic points in the rhythm; if the dancer used a step like the *Seguito spezzato* he would not be obliged to adjust to the change of beat.

The three canarios in Example 58, by Caroso (a), Zanetti (b), and Negri (c) respectively, all have the same rhythm, though it is expressed in quite different notations. The triple beats made up of groups of three semiminims in (a) correspond to groups of three black minims in the *emiolia* notation of (c), and the apparently duple notation of (b) would probably be adjusted to the triple meter in the manner suggested for Zanetti's corrente in Example 56.

FIVE

THE RELATION OF VERSE RHYTHM TO MUSICAL RHYTHM

The Nature of Italian Versification

THE COMPOSER WHO UNDERTAKES TO SET A STROPHIC POEM IS FACED WITH a very special problem. Quite apart from making the music suit the general mood of the poem, he must be careful not to violate seriously the prosody of any of the stanzas. In any poem that is not doggerel the rhythm and accentuation vary to some degree from stanza to stanza and even from line to line. It is therefore obviously impossible for the music to fit the corresponding lines of all the stanzas equally well. However, the composer will do the best he can to perform this impossible task—he will try to write music that will do violence to the least possible number of lines. To accomplish this he must find out which aspects of the prosody are variable and which remain constant from line to line and from stanza to stanza. He must be aware, whether consciously or not, of the rhythmic structure of the type of poem he is setting. Since the possibilities of musical rhythm are almost infinite, there is more than one way of adjusting it to fit any particular type of poetic meter. Nevertheless, the composers of the early seventeenth century found that certain types of musical rhythms worked out especially well in combination with certain types of Italian verse. These patterns became more or less stereotyped and were absorbed into the musical vocabulary of the Baroque period. Before investigating these patterns in detail it will be necessary to summarize the main principles of Italian versification and to define the general relationship that exists between verse rhythm and musical rhythm.

Italian versification is derived from classical Greek and Latin meters which, during the Middle Ages, underwent various modifications and transformations. The ancient Greeks possessed a high degree of sensitivity to the duration of sounds that enabled them to distinguish clearly between long and short syllables. Their poetry was devoid of accentuation as we know it; one syllable in every word was made prominent not through stress but through melodic emphasis, for Greek poetry was always sung. Long and short syllables were grouped in various ways to form *feet*, which constituted the metric units. Feet were so called because they corresponded to the intervals between successive *theses*, or moments when the feet touched the ground and regulated the rhythm of poetry, music, and dance. The theses of metrical feet coincided with the long syllables but not necessarily with the tonic accents of the words, which were distributed fortuitously. This discrepancy caused no rhythmic conflict for the Greeks because the disagreement was between duration on the one hand and pitch on the other.[1]

The Greek system of meter was imposed on the Latin language very early—probably in the second century B.C. by Ennius and Plautus. It governed Latin poetry throughout the classic era. When poetry was no longer sung and accents were expressed through dynamic stress the conflict between metric feet and word accent became a rhythmic problem that led eventually to accentual prosody and the destruction of the foot. The manner in which this came about is still a matter of controversy. We do not know just how meter and accents were reconciled when the following iambic trimeter by Catullus was recited:

◡ – ◡ – | ◡ – ◡ – | ◡ – ◡ –
Símul secúndus íncidísset in pédem

Grammatical accents may have been disregarded in favor of the ictus of the feet, or vice versa. Or perhaps some compromise was made, the nature of which we do not fully understand. We do know, however, that during the Middle Ages stress accents took on more and more importance in expressing the rhythm. They finally upset the balance between long and short syllables and caused a gradual weakening in the sense of duration. Classical verses were no longer read according to the rules of prosody. The grammatical accent became the true basis of rhythm for ears that could not easily distinguish

1. Cf. Thrasybulos Georgiades, *Greek Music, Verse, and Dance*, New York, n.d.

between long and short syllables. New Latin poets modeled their verses on those of the classics; in reading them however, they used the common pronunciation of words according to their grammatical accents, and they no longer measured their meters by feet but by number of syllables per line. Henceforth an iambic trimeter was nothing more than a twelve-syllable line with accents at specified intervals. In order to compensate for the weak and prosaic effect of rhythms governed solely by accent a new feature was added—rhyme. The function of rhyme is to strengthen and confirm the position of the thesis at the end (and sometimes also in the middle) of the line, where the voice arrives at a point of rest. Thus, in medieval Latin verse there already existed the three basic elements of Italian versification: (1) accent, (2) strict number of syllables, and (3) rhyme.

Italian versification, then, is both accentual and numerative. Strictly speaking, it cannot be called metrical since it is neither measured nor is it composed of groups of regularly recurring units. Italian writers on versification usually refer to the structure of the line as *ritmica*, reserving the term *metrica* for larger poetic structures, such as the *strofa*, in which the individual verse is used as a metric unit. The various kind of *ritmi* are distinguished by the position of the main tonic accents in relation to the number of syllables in each line. They are designated as follows in Italian treatises on versification:[2]

Quadernario, a four-syllable line with the principal accent on the third syllable.

Quinario, a five-syllable line with the primary accent on the fourth syllable.

Senario, a six-syllable line with the principal accent on the fifth syllable and a secondary accent on the second.

Settenario, a seven-syllable line with accents on the sixth syllable and one of the first four.

Ottonario, an eight-syllable line accented on the third and seventh syllables with a caesura after the third or the fourth syllable.

Novenario, a nine-syllable line accented on the second, fifth, and eighth or on the third, sixth, and eighth syllables.

Decasillabo, a ten-syllable line with accents on the third, sixth, and ninth.

---

2. Cf. for example: Rocco Murari, *Ritmica e metrica razionale italiana*, Milan, 1900; Pasquale Leonetti, *Storia della tecnica del verso italiano*, Rome, 1933; Vincenzo Pernicone, *Storia e svolgimento della metrica*, Milan, 1948; Paulo Rossi, *Metrica italiana e classica*, Milan, 1949; Domenico Magri, *Armoniosi accenti*, Turin, 1956.

Endecasillabo, an eleven-syllable line with accents on the sixth and tenth, on the fourth, eighth, and tenth, or on the fourth, seventh, and tenth, depending on the position of the caesura.

The number of syllables per line being one of the basic factors of Italian prosody, it is important that there be no doubt as to the method of counting them. Since the theoretical number of syllables in a line for purposes of versification does not always coincide with the actual number of syllables in the spoken or written words, a number of conventions have been established that help determine just which syllables should be counted. In the first place feminine endings—those with accents on penultimate syllables—are preponderant to such an extent that anything else is considered exceptional. All lines, therefore, are counted as though there were one syllable after the final accent in which case the line is called *verso piano;* if there be two the final word is called *sdrucciola;* if there be none the final word is *tronca* or truncated. The following lines, for instance, are all regarded as *settenari* although the second actually has eight syllables and the third only six:

Hor-mai la Not-t' in gí-ro (*piano*)
Dall' al-trui mal si rí-do-no (*sdrucciolo*)
Pa-stor le-va-te sù (*tronco*)

The number of syllables per line is further modified by the so-called "metrical figures": (1) Elision is the dropping or partial pronunciation of a vowel when a word ends with a vowel and the following word begins with a vowel; the final of the first word and the initial of the next are elided and counted as a single syllable. Example:

Pas-to-rel-la‿o-ve ti‿as-con-di (eight syllables)
1 2 3 4 5 6 7 8

(2) Diaeresis occurs when consecutive vowels of a single syllable are pronounced separately. This is often indicated by two dots over one of the vowels. Example:

Qua-le ne' ple-ri-clu-ni-ï se-re-ni (eleven syllables)
1 2 3 4 5 6 7 8 9 10 11

Tri-vï-a ri-de tra le nin-fe‿e-ter-ne (eleven syllables)
1 2 3 4 5 6 7 8 9 10 11

A word ending in two or more vowels forms diaeresis when it comes at the end of a line, whereas in the course of a line the vowels form a single syllable. Example:

S'io	ti	mi-ro	fil-li	mi-ä	(eight syllables)
1	2	3 4	5 6	7 8	

Al-ma	mia	do-ve	t'en	va-i	(eight syllables)
1 2	3	4 5	6	7 8	

(3) Hiatus, the opposite of elision, is the separation of a vowel that ends one word from a vowel beginning the next. It usually occurs when one or both of the vowels in question are accented, as:

E	tu	che	se'	cos-tì	a-ni-ma	vi-va	(eleven syllables)
1	2	3	4	5 6	7 8 9	10 11	

E	poì	che	tut-ti	si	sen-tì	a	gio-co	(eleven syllables)
1	2	3	4 5	6	7 8	9	10 11	

or when three vowels come together:

Che‿a-ve-te	tu	e‿il	tuo	pa-dre	sof-fer-to	(eleven syllables)
1 2 3	4	5	6	7 8	9 10 11	

One further point may be mentioned here in connection with the conventions that are taken for granted in Italian versification. This is the existence of several degrees of rhyme. Strictly speaking, rhyme must be defined as the identity of final syllables beginning with the accented vowel, as: p*etto*, t*etto*, pargol*etto*, sogg*etto*. In practice, however, strict rhyme is sometimes replaced by two forms of *assonance:* (1) the identity of the accented vowels and the final unaccented vowels, as: *a*cqu*a*, f*a*tt*a*; b*e*n*e*, n*e*r*e*, and (2) the identity of the last consonants and the final unaccented vowels, as: colo*re*, ma*re*.

Several attempts have been made to define the relationship between verse rhythms and musical rhythms. Emilia Fiorentino, in an article entitled "The Rhythms of Italian Poetry Are Musical Rhythms," [3] asserts that they are identical. "The close affinity between the two rhythms," she writes, "seemed to me so certain that I resolved to undertake a study of Italian poetic meters using musical rhythm as my sole guide." Sra. Fiorentino finds the conventional terminology for verse rhythms inadequate and believes that definitions couched in musical terms would reveal the true rhythms of the verses. Adhering to the principle that the syllables of Italian verse are all the same length, she allots an eighth note or a quarter note to each syllable, places the barlines before accented syllables, and arrives at results like the following:

---

3. E. Fiorentino, "I Ritmi della poesia italiana sono quelli della musica," *Rivista Musicale Italiana*, XXIII, fasc. 2, 1916.

Ottonario: occupies two measures of $\frac{2}{4}$ time. each verse beginning in the middle of a measure.

Gia le-va-te su gli spal-le ¦ De' ca-stel-li sub-al-pi-ni

Senario: two measures of $\frac{3}{8}$.

sul chiu-so qua-der-no ¦ Di va-ti fa-mo-si

Settenario: two measures of $\frac{4}{4}$.

La guan-cia ri-sor-gen-te ¦ Ton-deg-gia sul bel vi-so

At the time of writing her article, Sra. Fiorentino did not have access to Zambaldi's *Il ritmo dei versi*[4] (Turin, 1882) wherein a similar theory is propounded. Zambaldi proceeds in a much more scholarly fashion. He traces the derivation of each type of Italian verse to its source in a corresponding Greek or Latin meter. In translating the rhythms into musical notation he allows for the prolongation of the accented syllable (thesis) and a longer duration for the syllable preceding the caesura. Since he uses two different note values his results inevitably differ from Fiorentino's. A comparison of his interpretations with those quoted above proves interesting:

Ottonario: two measures of $\frac{3}{4}$:

Senario: two measures of $\frac{2}{4}$:

Tor-ren-te cre-sciu-to ¦ Per tor-bi-da pie-na

Settenario: two measures of $\frac{6}{8}$:

The two versions are seen to be not only different but contradictory, in that what is triple meter for one author is duple meter for the other. The amazing thing is, however, that in spite of these contradictions *all* the versions

4. According to her own statement in the above-mentioned article.

of both writers fit the prosody of the texts; all are good musical settings that have actually been used at some time or another by reputable composers. This fact alone should be enough to prove that both theories are unsound, at least as far as the exclusivity of their interpretations is concerned. Actually, the basic approach of our two authors is the same: they both impose arbitrary meters upon verse rhythms. This is also the procedure followed by a third writer, Tacchinardi,[5] who deals with poetic verses from the point of view of musical rhythm and arrives at still different but equally plausible results.

The conclusion that can be drawn from all this is that verse rhythms are in themselves non-metrical but are susceptible to being adapted to various meters. In order to ascertain the true nature of these rhythms let us return to our original definition of rhythm and try to find out what kind of rhythm has no metrical basis but is not averse to having meter thrust upon it. Rhythm is "the act of organizing recurring events in time." In metric rhythm the events to be organized—the *rhythmizomena*—are metric units: measured feet in the case of ancient Greek music and poetry; pulses, beats, and measures in the case of Western music. In the accentual rhythm of Italian verse the events to be organized are groups composed of accented syllables preceded and followed by specified numbers of indeterminate syllables that may or may not be accented. The rhythms cannot exist on the printed page. To be organized in time, "rhythmized," the elements of rhythm symbolized by the printed words must be given concrete existence through sound. Sound implies duration, and the first question that must be answered relates to the duration of sound of accented and unaccented syllables when *spoken*, not sung.

The theory that the syllables of Italian verse are isochronous is not only an oversimplification but is downright false. The evidence is all on the other side. One has only to listen to the ordinary speech of Italians to become aware that they tend to dwell on accented syllables. Some accented syllables, moreover, are dwelt upon longer than others. An open vowel, for instance, is longer than a vowel followed by a double consonant (*vita*, *vitta*), and an accented penultimate is longer than an accented final (*lontano*, *città*). From the point of view of relative duration it may even be said that Italian has its iambs (*volar*, *omai*), its trochees (*carne*, *passo*), its spondees (*portan*, *causar*) its dactyls (*dattilo*, *timpano*), its anapaests (*riderem*, *morirai*), its amphibrachs (*vederlo*, *vedesti*).[6] The apparent similarity of such ready-made

5. Alberto Tacchinardi, *Ritmica musicale*, 2nd ed. Milan, 1926.
6. Cf. Francesco d'Ovidio, "La versificazione delle ode barbare," *Versificazione Romanza*, Naples, 1932.

combinations of longs and shorts to classical feet encouraged many poets to write Italian verse in imitation of old Greek and Latin metrical forms. This *poesia barbara*, as Carducci calls it, was doubtless inspired by the desire of Renaissance humanists to recapture their ancient heritage.[7] After the first attempts by Leonardo Dati and Leon Battista Alberti in the fifteenth century, Claudio Tolomei formulated rules for this technique in his *Versi et regole della nuova poesia italiana* (1535).

The reform of the Tuscan lyric at the beginning of the seventeenth century was brought about largely through Chiabrera's study of Greek models. That it was given a strong impetus by the exigencies of the new music is attested by Jacopo Peri in the preface to his *Musiche* of 1600. According to Carducci Peri states that his dissatisfaction with the kinds of texts used by the musicians of the previous generation led him to search for canzonette that would give him more opportunity for variety in composing airs to be sung to the accompaniment of stringed instruments. His needs, he says, were best fulfilled by the verses of Signor Gabriello Chiabrera.[8]

The novelty of reform was not so much the imitation of classical meters as the introduction through them of verse forms other than the *endecasillabo* and the *settenario*, which had held almost exclusive sway for a long period. This new rhythmic variety, which characterized the Italian lyric from then on, had the further effect of reconciling the poets and patrons to popular verse forms that had been disdained in the sixteenth century. Sporadic attempts to use Greek meters in Italian verse continued through the ensuing centuries and finally culminated in Carducci's *Ode barbari.* According to the best authorities the most successful writers of *poemi barbari* have avoided the conflict of rhythm and meter by a) placing accented syllables on the theses of metric feet, or b) choosing from among the classical meters those which can be reproduced by means of long and short syllables within the

---

7. Cf. Giosuè Carducci, *La Poesia barbara*, Bologna, 1881, and "Dello svolgimento dell'ode in Italia," *Prose di Giosuè Carducci*, Bologna, 1933.

8. Jacopo Peri, *Le Musiche*, Florence, 1600: "Considerato che altresí in quei tempi si usavano per i musici alcune canzonette per lo piú di parole vili, le quali pareva a me che non si convenissero e che tra gli uomini intendenti non si stimassero; mi venne anco pensiero, per sollevamento talvolta degli animi oppressi, comporre qualche canzonetta a uso di aria per poter usare in concerto di piú strumenti a corda: e communicato questo mio pensiero a molti gentiluomini della città, fui compiaciuto cortesemente da essi di molte canzonette di misure varie di versi; si come anche appresso dal signor Gabriello Chiabrera, che in molta copia et assai diversificata da tutte le altre, ne fui favorito, prestandomi egli grande occasione di andar variando: le quali tutte composte da me in diverse arie di tempo in tempo state non sono poi disagiate eziandio a tutta Italia" (Prefaz. ai lettori). Quoted by Carducci, in "Dello svolgimento dell'ode in Italia," *Prose di Giosue Carducci*, p. 1414.

framework of Italian verses or coupled verses.[9] Nevertheless it must be admitted that no matter how carefully long and short syllables are adjusted to the long and short positions in Greek meters, Italian verses can never become metrical for the very simple reason that the durations of Italian syllables are not measured.

Granted that long and short syllables do exist in Italian, the question *how much* longer the long is than the short cannot be answered by naming a ratio 2:1 or 1½:1, as it can be in the case of Greek syllables. If we examine the durations of Italian syllables a little more closely we find that not only is one long syllable longer than another long syllable but that the *same* long syllable may be longer or shorter according to the particular situation. One can say "madre," "maadre," or "maaadre." The length of the syllable "ma" does not depend solely on its position as a grammatical accent but upon many other factors as well: the meaning of the word, its syntactical position in the sentence, its emotional connotation for the speaker, even the speaker's personality and the regional speech of his place of origin. The same is true of the shortness of short syllables. It is evident, then, that the Italian syllable has no fixed duration but is *given* a duration on each separate occasion by the speaker, who makes it longer or shorter as he pleases. It is this subjective variability of durations, indeed, that makes it possible to set Italian verse to music. The composer replaces the speaker and bestows metrical, instead of purely linguistic, durations upon the syllables. As Georgiades points out, this is the crucial difference between Western verse and Greek verse. All Greek drama was sung; but since the rhythm and pitch level were already inherent in the syllables the poet, in selecting the words, had already "composed" the music.[10]

The rhythm of Italian verse, then, does not depend upon fixed durations of sound. Yet the essence of rhythm is the organization of sounds in time. How can sounds be organized in time if they have no precise duration? The only possible answer to this paradox is that the rhythm is created afresh every time the verse is uttered. The verse on the printed page does not contain the rhythm but only a plan for a rhythm—a plan that may be brought to fulfillment in many different ways. The plan itself is quite definite. It consists of a certain number of syllables, a fixed order of accentuation, and a specified number of syllables between the accents. A *quinario* may be represented thus: . . . .′ . , an *ottonario* thus: . . .′ . . . .′ . The accent stands for a point of emphasis. But it is a mistake to think of the plan as static. The accented

9. Cf. Francesco d'Ovidio, *op. cit.*
10. T. Georgiades, *op. cit.*, Chapter IV.

syllable does not arrive like a sudden *sforzando* in the midst of an undifferentiated succession of sounds. A well-built verse is dynamic; its syllables are not stationary but in motion, progressing toward a peak. In terms of motion and repose the accented syllable represents a point of arrival. If it is a final syllable it is also a point of repose, a thetic point, as in the *quinario tronco:*

A A A T
non t'a-me-rò

More often, because of the preponderance of paroxytone words in Italian, the accented syllable is followed by another syllable that concludes the verse or the hemistich. This syllable, upon which the voice comes to a momentary pause, is more thetic than the accented syllable that preceded it. The accented syllable, in this case, corresponds to what we have called rhythmic climax in our analysis of dance rhythms; it is a point of arrival in relation to the preceding syllables but it is also a point of departure toward the final thetic syllable:

A A A X T
La-dra d'a-mó-re

By applying the principles of arsis and thesis we have now arrived at a means of analyzing the rhythms of Italian verse without regard to the durations of the syllables. Such an analysis is, of course, schematic. To produce a concrete rhythm the scheme must still be filled in with physical sounds, each of which has its attributes of pitch, duration, and intensity. The reader may wonder why this sort of scheme is any more useful than a scheme of accents and numbers. The answer is twofold. In the first place, motion and repose are more basic to rhythm than are accents and numbers, or even pitch, duration, and intensity, for these qualities are only the physical means through which the rhythm is communicated. Secondly, we have already discovered something about the functions of motion and repose in musical rhythm, so we shall now have a basis for comparison which was lacking when we were dealing only with accents and numbers.

Before going any further it will be profitable to consider just what is meant by the term "accent" in the rhythmic scheme. Is accent necessarily to be equated with dynamic stress or intensity? It may be assumed that in general an accented syllable is delivered with more force than an unaccented syllable. In the rhythmic schemes of verses the positions of the "principal" accents are fixed. There may be other accented syllables in the verse; a *quinario,* for example, may begin with an accented syllable: .′ . . .′ . , but only the fourth is a "principal" accent. Does this mean that the fourth syllable is to be louder than the first? Not necessarily. You may say "*La*dra d'amore" or "Ladra d'a*mo*re," depending on whether you want to emphasize the fact that she is a *thief* or the fact that *love* is what she is stealing. In either case the "principal" rhythmic accent is the fourth syllable, not because it is louder but because it is a point of arrival in the flow of movement. Intensity, in this case, is one of the attributes of a particular interpretation, just as duration is. You may say "Laaadra d'amore" or "Ladra d'amooore" without altering the basic rhythm of the verse. The same thing is true of pitch; either the first or the fourth syllable may be spoken with a higher intonation, producing different interpretations of the same rhythm.

The term "accent," then, is used in two senses; on the one hand it is associated with dynamic stress, on the other it may refer to a purely rhythmic emphasis as a point of arrival. In the latter sense accent has a close affinity with the thesis of the musical beat or measure. The similar functions of the two phenomena may be used to define more precisely the relationship between verse rhythm and musical rhythm.

The reader will remember that "beat" was defined as a metrical unit formed by grouping two or three pulses, and that the pulse that is perceived as a focal point of the beat is called the thesis. In verse rhythm there are no pulses or beats; nevertheless the accented syllables may be regarded as focal points toward which the unaccented syllables lead. The process of setting verse to music starts by assigning metrical qualities to the successive syllables of the verse. Whether the individual syllable becomes a pulse, a beat, or a group of beats depends upon the duration that the composer decides to bestow upon it. But he must see to it that the metric unit that he allots to the syllable retains the arsic or thetic quality in relation to the rest of the syllables of the verse. If syllables are converted into pulses the accented syllables should fall on thetic pulses of beats. If syllables are converted into beats, then the accented syllables should fall on thetic beats of the measure. The "principal" accent of the verse should fall on the beat that represents the rhythmic climax of the musical phrase. The various levels of meter in musical rhythm also have their equivalents in verse rhythm. Just as a thetic point on one level of meter may be arsic on a higher level, an accented syllable, which is thetic in respect to an unaccented syllable, may be arsic in respect to another accented syllable.

Varied durations assigned to syllables by the composer have an interpretive effect on the music similar to that of varied durations in speech. A tone may be prolonged to emphasize a thetic point; it is not the prolongation, however, that makes the tone thetic, but its rhythmic position in the phrase.

These principles of analysis will now be applied to specific examples in an attempt to define some of the musico-poetic rhythmic patterns that are most characteristic of early Baroque music.

OTTONARIO RHYTHMS

ITALIAN VERSES fall into two categories according to whether or not they are divisible into equal parts. The first category comprises *senario*, *ottonario*, and *decasillabo*, the second *quinario*, *settenario*, and *endecasillabo*. This seems like an arbitrary classification, but it is actually functional in respect to the rhythmic structure of the poem. Every Italian verse has its primary accent on the penultimate syllable. When the verse is divisible into equal parts the accent tends to fall on the penultimate syllable of each part, so that the verse appears to be composed of a number of equal hemistichs. The *ottonario* divides into two *quaternarii*, the *senario* into two three-syllable kernels, each of which has its obligatory accent on the penultimate. This process, moreover, tends to carry over into the larger divisions of the structure; two *ottonarii* are often coupled to form a sixteen-syllable period, the fifteenth syllable of which becomes the point of arrival for the whole rhythm. The primary accents of the smaller components become the secondary accents of the larger, with the result that this class of verse tends to have a more regular rhythmic structure with a greater number of fixed accents than does the class comprising the *quinario*, *settenario*, and *endecasillabo*. The structural regularity of *ottonario* stanzas bears a marked resemblance to the regularity we have observed in the larger metric structure of dance pieces. It is not surprising to find that the *ottonario* was the favorite verse rhythm of the composers who wrote for court entertainments wherein the dance played an important role. It outnumbers all other types of verse by about four to one during the period with which we are concerned.

The text and music of Brunelli's *Nelle vaghe trece* illustrates the kind of cumulative structure that is often engendered by *ottonario* rhythms:

A	A	A	X	A	A	A	T
A	T	A	T	A	T	A	T
′	′	′	′	′	′	′	′
Nelle	vaghe	trece	bionde	Di voi	donn'e	nel bel	volto

A A A X A A A T
A T A T A T A T
Tutto lieto s'e raccolto Ne' vostr'occhi si nasconde

A A A X A A A X A A A T
A T A T A T A T A T A T
Ivi loco e tempo aspetta Piglia l'arco e poi saetta Piglia l'arco e poi saetta

Every odd-numbered syllable is accented, as in Longfellow's trochaic tetrameter. In Brunelli's syllabic setting each pair of syllables is treated as a metric beat, with the accented syllable on the thesis. One *ottonario* verse occupies four beats, of which the first and third are arsic to the second and fourth (A T A *T*). But since the primary accent of the verse falls on the seventh syllable the second beat is less thetic than the fourth and becomes a rhythmic climax in relation to it (A X A T). If the movement continues without interruption at the fourth beat, that beat in turn becomes a rhythmic climax in relation to the eighth beat (fifteenth syllable): (A A A X A A A T). This rhythmic pattern is repeated for the next two *ottonarii*, and finally repeated again, but extended to twelve beats (24 syllables) by the repeated text of the final verse.

EX. 59 BRUNELLI, 1616 *p.28*

In this piece Brunelli is adapting the *ottonario* verse to the dance rhythm of the corrente, which, as we have seen, proceeds in groups of four fast triple beats (cf. Ex. 37c of Chapter IV). His notation, under the signature C $^{6}_{4}$, calls for two triple beats per tactus, implying a rapid tempo. Since the tactus always starts with a downstroke there is no way of indicating in this notation that the first beat is arsic to the second. The music itself does show, by other means, that the 4th, 8th, 12th, and 16th beats are thetic points. On each of these beats a harmonic cadence takes place; the bass ascends a fourth or descends a fifth, and a suspension dissonance occurs on the preceding beat, as may be seen in Example 59, where the figured bass specifies the harmony. In modern notation the continuous alternation of arsic and thetic beats could be shown by means of a $\frac{6}{8}$ meter starting on the second half of the measure:

$\frac{6}{8}$ 𝄾 ♩ ♪ | ♩ ♪ ♩ ♪ | ♩ ♪ (A T A T)

Still more explicit, however, is a $\frac{12}{8}$ measure, which implies that the fourth beat is more thetic than the second:

$\frac{12}{8}$ 𝄾 ♩ ♪ ♩ ♪ ♩ ♪ | ♩ ♪ (A X A T)

This is the notation used for the transcription of the entire piece in the Anthology at the end of this volume. It still, of course, is unable to convey the information that the fourth beat is a rhythmic climax in relation to the eighth.

The rhythmic pattern just described, which may be called the *ottonario-corrente* rhythm, is often modified in a number of ways—especially in songs where the continuous motion of the dance is not desired—in order to make the thetic points more explicit. Visconti, in his *Cruda Filli*, for instance, places a rest after the fourth beat to indicate the articulation at the end of the line. At the same time he cuts short the first note of the phrase, thus eliminating the metric accent on the first syllable, which in most *ottonario* verses is superfluous and even misleading since the third syllable bears a stronger accent than the first. (See Ex. 60; a is the original notation, b the author's transcription.)

EX. 60

VISCONTI *p.8*

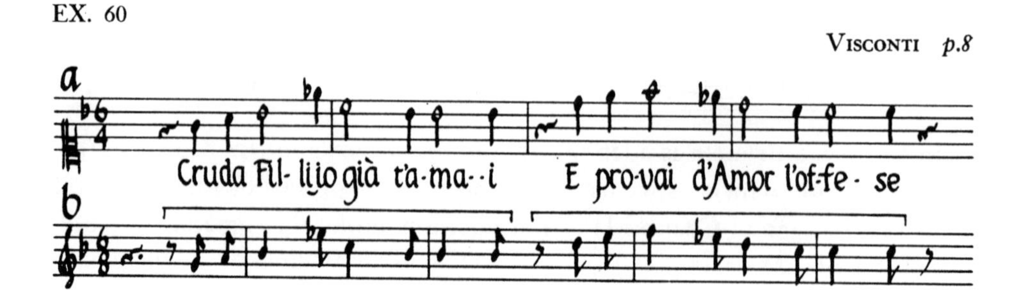

The thetic quality of the final syllable of the line may be emphasized by prolonging the last note, in place of inserting a rest. In this case the final note becomes a beat instead of a pulse. But it is a duple, not a triple beat, and therefore results in a hemiola rhythm, the last two syllables of the verse and the first two of the succeeding verse forming a measure of three duple beats that alternates with the measure of two triple beats occupied by the central portion of the verse. This rhythm, as we have seen in Chapter III, could be expressed in the notation of the period under the signatures C, C $^{6}_{4}$, C $^{3}_{2}$, or by indicating the duple beats by means of black notes, as in the Magliabecchiana MS version of Caccini's *Non ha'l cielo* (Ex. 61). In any case it is best rendered in modern notation by $^{6}_{4}$ or an alternation of $^{6}_{8}$ and $^{3}_{4}$ measures, as shown in the transcriptions of Caccini's song (Ex. 61b) and of Visconti's *Pastorella ove t'ascondi* (Ex. 62).

The five-beat *ottonario-hemiola* is one of the favorite patterns of the Baroque period but it is often obscured by a notation that does not show the change of beat. Since two of the five beats are triple and the other three are duple a conflict of beat-versus-tactus is inevitable, whether the latter be of the *aequalis* or the *inaequalis* variety. The tactus called for by the signature does, however, have some implications in regard to tempo. Three degrees of speed are implied by the signatures C $^{3}_{2}$, C, and C $^{6}_{4}$, because the duration of the total pattern under the first signature is four tactus, under the second signature three tactus, and under the third only two tactus. Perhaps the simplest way to clarify this relationship would be to coordinate the twelve pulses of the pattern, which in terms of beats are grouped 2.3.3.2.2, with the tactus called for by each signature. The reader will recall that C $\frac{3}{2}$ demands three minim pulses per tactus, the signature C two minim pulses per tactus, and C $\frac{6}{4}$ six semiminim pulses per tactus. The distribution, then, will be as follows:

C $\frac{3}{2}$ equals 4 tactus

C equals 3 tactus

C $\frac{6}{4}$ equals 2 tactus

modern notation

Even though the speed of the tactus was not standardized at this time, a pattern that takes twice as many tactus to perform under one signature as it did under a previous signature can be assumed to move at a slower tempo.

If the two triple beats in the center of the hemiola rhythm are converted into three duple beats the result is a pattern of six duple beats with theses on the second and fifth:

1 2 3 4 5

Although almost invariably notated under the signature C, this pattern falls naturally into two measures of slow $\frac{3}{4}$ meter, beginning on the third beat of the measure and ending on the second. This is the metric pattern in $\frac{3}{4}$ time that Zambaldi identifies with the *ottonario* verse (cf. supra p. 108) on the grounds that it divides the verse into two equal *quaternarii*. It is frequently used, but very rarely without some modification of the note values. The *ottonario* verse is symmetrical as far as accentuation is concerned, but whereas the last two syllables are always relatively thetic the fourth often is not, especially when the caesura occurs after the third syllable. Composers therefore lengthen the note on the second beat (which bears the third syllable), postponing the fourth syllable to the arsis. The second beat then becomes a rhythmic climax, the fifth and sixth remaining thetic. The note on the sixth syllable is also frequently shortened to emphasize the thetic quality of the seventh:

Examples 63, 64, and 65 illustrate this pattern; it will be noted that in each case there is a caesura after the third syllable. In Example 64, by Brunelli, the emphasis on the second beat is effected through a melisma instead of a longer duration; the use of ornamentation for this purpose is a very common practice. This example, incidentally, contains a single *quaternario*, "L'alte

EX. 63

EX. 66

MONTEVERDI in BARBERA *fol.32*

lodi," between the two *ottonarii.* Marco da Gagliano injects an interesting rhythmic subtlety in his setting of *Alma mia* (Ex. 65) by syncopating the irregular accent on the first syllable of *dove.* Example 66 is the beginning of an aria from Monteverdi's *Orfeo* as it appears in the Barbera MS. Here we find that the composer has fused two *ottonario* lines by inserting a single measure of two triple beats into a rhythm that basically conforms to the six-beat pattern.

The *ottonario* verse is also frequently adapted to patterns of four duple beats by allotting a pair of syllables to each beat. When the signature C is used, as is generally the case, two different tempos can be specified: a rapid tempo in which each syllable is sung to an eighth note, as in Example 67, or a moderate tempo in which the basic value of each syllable is a semiminim, as in Example 68. In the former case the pattern occupies a single tactus; in the latter it takes the time of two tactus. Pesenti, in *Qui vedrò quel chiaro sole* (Ex. 67) gives all the syllables the same duration; his pattern is identical with Sra. Fiorentino's definition of the musical rhythm of the *ottonario.* This is unrealistic, as we have seen, but Pesenti uses it because his song accompanies a rapid dance that requires continuous motion.

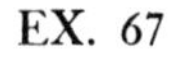
EX. 67

PESENTI

Much more characteristic *ottonario* settings are those in which some syllables are lengthened and others shortened in accordance with their rhythmic functions in the verse. In Brunelli's *Donzellette vezzosette* (Ex. 68), for instance, the lengthening of the first syllable of *vezzosette* produces a rhythmic climax on the third beat; at the same time the shortened arsis on the second syllable emphasizes the thetic quality of the fourth beat. The accent on the first syllable of the verse is minimized by postponing it to the arsis of the beat. The first syllable of the second verse is *not* shortened, for *Deh'* (Alas!) needs more emphasis.

EX. 68

BRUNELLI, 1614 *p.15*

The notes on the two final syllables of the *ottonario* are often lengthened to clarify the articulations between the lines. In this case the four-beat pattern is extended to five, or even more beats, with the result that a transcription using regularly placed barlines will inevitably distort the rhythm. In order to retain the barlines before the third and seventh syllables of the verse, changes of time signature must be introduced. Examples 69 and 70 demonstrate that if these changes are judiciously placed, the rhythmic patterns are

EX. 69

BRUNELLI, 1616 *p.11*

EX. 70

VITALI *p.7*

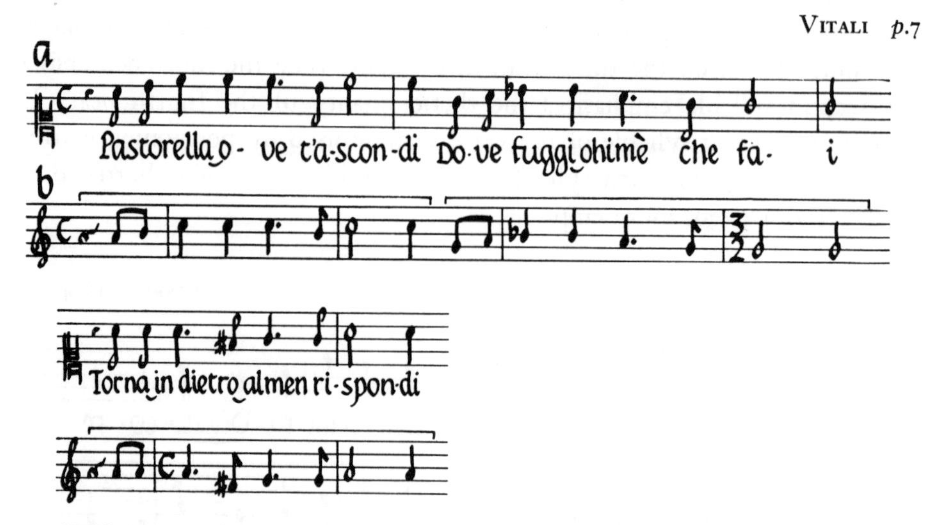

remarkably clear in spite of their irregular spacing.

The eight syllables of the *ottonario* verse do not easily adjust themselves to the six-beat gagliarda rhythm, but Brunelli's dance song, *Del bel Arno* (Ex. 71) illustrates two ways in which this can be accomplished. The first verse is spread out to embrace the twelve beats of two *tempi di gagliarda* by lengthening the first syllable to two beats, and the third, with ornamentation, to three. The second and third verses are syllabic, each being adjusted to one *tempo di gagliarda* by allotting one beat to each of the first three pairs of syllables. The two final syllables of all three verses conform to the normal phrase ending that accompanies the *cadenza.*

EX. 71

BRUNELLI, 1616 *p.16*

QUINARIO RHYTHMS

THE NORMAL recitation of a *quinario* line, with a slight prolongation of the fourth syllable to emphasize the primary accent, is a very close approximation to the basic six-beat rhythm of the gagliarda. The five syllables correspond to the five movements of the *cinque passi* and the rhythmic climax on the fourth syllable resembles the take-off for the *cadenza.* One finds, indeed, that a large majority of the musical settings of the *quinario* falls into the gagliarda pattern. The most common notation is also the same as that generally used for the gagliarda—*sesquialtera minore,* $^{3}_{2}$C, with three minims to the tactus. (See Ex. 72a.) A transcription in $^{6}_{4}$, beginning the pattern on the second half of the measure, will put the primary accent in an appropriate metrical position (Ex. 72b). When the pattern appears under C $^{6}_{4}$ in the original notation a faster tempo is indicated, as we have seen in the case of Visconti's *Non vuoi ch'io t'ami.* (See Chapter III, Exx. 25 and 26.)

EX. 72

BUCCHIANTI *p.22*

Calestani, in *O luci belle* (Ex. 73) uses the *sesquialtera maggiore,* ₵$^{3}_{2}$, with three semibreves per tactus. It will be seen that the first two *quinarii* are fused through the prolongation of the second *O,* which produces a hemiola rhythm similar to that found in the fusion of two *tempi di gagliarda.* This twelve-beat pattern is used whenever pairs of *quinarii* are coupled to form *decasillabi,* as in Bucchianti's *Leggeadra Rosa de' Fior Regina* (Ex. 74).

EX. 73

CALESTANI *p.42*

EX. 74

BUCCHIANTI *p.23*

The secondary accent of the *quinario* usually falls upon the first syllable of the line. In the settings discussed so far this accent coincides with the thesis of the first triple beat on the higher level of the gagliarda rhythm (the first dotted half note beat in the transcriptions). When the *second* syllable of the *quinario* bears the secondary accent the musical pattern must begin with an upbeat, so the normal gagliarda rhythm will not express the correct accentuation. G. B. da Gagliano's setting of *Pupille arciere* (Ex. 75a) is a case in point. Here the pattern is compressed into three beats. Each syllable is represented by a semiminim pulse, the second and fourth coinciding with the theses of the second and third beats. In transcription a triple meter should be used—either  $\frac{3}{4}$, as in Example 75b, or $\frac{3}{2}$ without reduction of note values. The barlines must, of course, be adjusted to precede the fourth syllable.

EX. 75

G. B. GAGLIANO *p.18*

If the last two syllables are prolonged the pattern will occupy four beats and the meter will become duple, as in the last three *quinarii* of Visconti's *Ladra d'amore*, which starts off in the gagliarda rhythm and shifts to this four-beat pattern by means of a change of signature (Ex. 76). In the last phrase of this song Visconti extends the pattern still further, giving two beats each to the fourth and fifth syllables (Ex. 77).

EX. 76

VISCONTI *p.8*

EX. 77

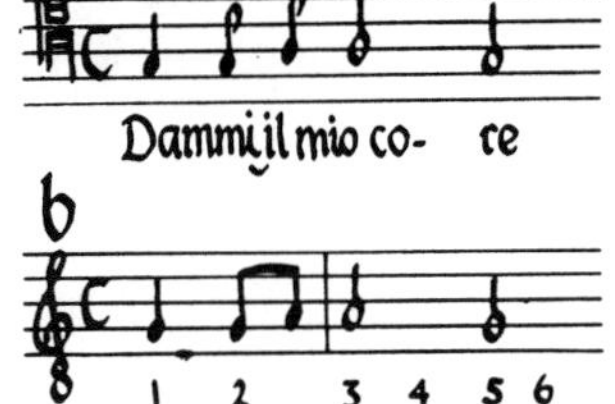

SENARIO RHYTHMS

THE *senario* line, with its accents on the second and fourth syllables, divides into two equal kernels of three syllables each. As in the case of the *ottonario* this regularity is usually carried into the larger metrical structure of the stanza, which consists of pairs of *senarii* that form twelve-syllable lines. When adapted to triple beats each syllable is given a pulse, the first being, of course, an upbeat. This results in a corrente rhythm of four beats to each pair of *senarii*. The most common setting of the *senario* is illustrated in G. B. da Gagliano's *Gioite, gioite* (Ex. 78a). This is definitely a dance rhythm that

EX. 78

G. B. GAGLIANO *p.36*

flows evenly in a regular succession of arsic and thetic beats. The even-numbered thetic beats are stronger than the others, since they coincide with the primary accents of the twelve-syllable lines. A transcription in $\frac{6}{8}$ meter should therefore begin on an arsic beat, as in Example 78b.

The *senario* is not often set to duple beats. *Fidele d'Amore*, an anonymous song in the Barbera MS, furnishes one example of such a setting. The basic meter is a succession of amphibrachs that correspond to the three-syllable kernels:

It is modified by a syncopation on the final syllable of each *senario*, which gives a strong emphasis to the penultimate syllable even though it is not lengthened (see Ex. 79).

EX. 79

SETTENARIO RHYTHMS

The *settenario* verse has its primary accent on the sixth syllable; secondary accents may fall on the second and fourth, the first and third, or the first and fourth, in that order of prevalence.

If a *settenario* with accents on the second, fourth, and sixth syllables is to be adjusted to metrical beats in such a way that the accented syllables coincide with the theses of beats, the rhythmic pattern must obviously begin with an upbeat. When the penultimate beat is lengthened the pattern will occupy four beats, which may be either triple, as in Example 80, or duple, as in Example 81. The pattern of four triple beats corresponds to the *corrente* rhythm; Calestani's *Accorta lusinghiera* (Ex. 80) bears, in fact, the superscript *In corrente*. The difference between the *ottonario-corrente* and the *settenario-corrente* rhythms is that in the former the thesis falls on the fourth beat (A A A T) while in the latter the thesis or rhythmic climax falls on the third beat (A A X T or A A T T), which corresponds to the primary accent of the verse, as can be seen in Calestani's song. Like the *ottonario-corrente* this pattern fits a $\frac{12}{8}$ meter, but in transcription the barline should precede the third beat instead of the fourth (see Ex. 80b).

Brunelli's *Non havea Febo ancora* illustrates the setting of *settenario* lines to four duple beats (Ex. 81). As in the triple-beat pattern the rhythmic climax or thesis falls on the third beat. A transcription in $\frac{4}{2}$ time with the bar line preceding this beat will be found to be rhythmically precisely analogous to the $\frac{12}{8}$ transcription of the corrente pattern. It suggests a slower tempo, as does the relationship of C to C^{6}_{4} in the original notations. The second verse of his text being truncated, Brunelli places a rest on the thesis of the fourth beat. Neither this nor the shortening of the second syllable of *mondo* causes any important alteration in the basic rhythm.

Sabatini's *Per due vezzosi lumi* is quoted in extenso in Example 82 to illustrate variations that often occur in *settenario* stanzas. The first two verses are regular, except that Sabatini omits the preliminary semibreve rest, so that the first measure of the transcription has only three beats instead of four. The third verse is truncated, then extended by the *quinario* "il vago errore";

these two verses together actually form an *endecasillabo* line. The last verse of the stanza, with an echo repetition, is used as a refrain. Sabatini sets this off from the preceding lines by changing the meter to the triple-beat pattern, which, however, he abbreviates to three beats by cutting short the two final syllables.

EX. 82

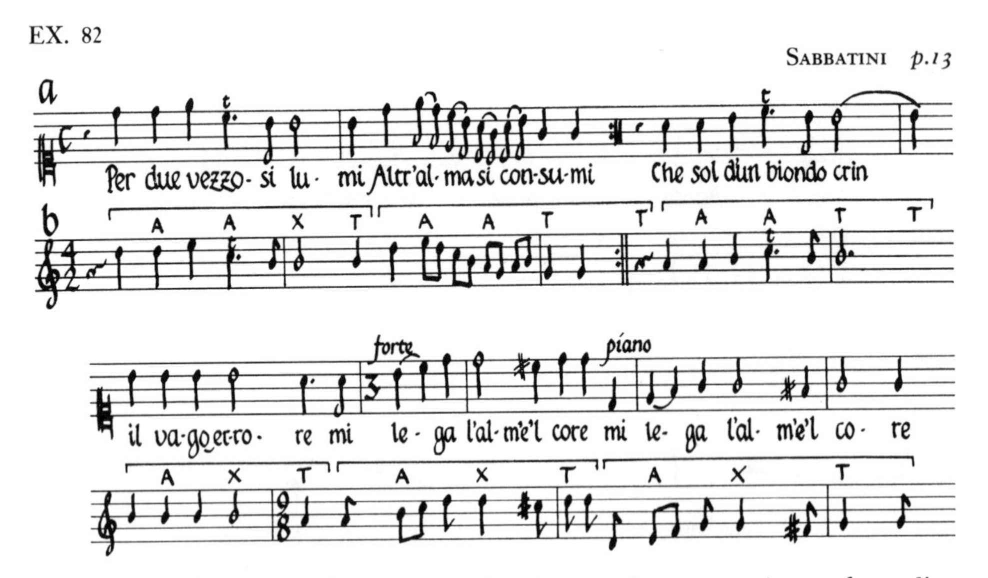

In *settenario* stanzas the accentuation is not always consistent from line to line. The anonymous song *O che felice giorno* from the Barbera manuscript contains examples of all three species of *settenario* (Ex. 83): line 1 has secondary accents on the first and fourth syllables, line 2 on the first and third, line 3 on the second and fourth, line 4 on the first and fourth. Lines in which the first syllable is accented obviously require no upbeat in the musical setting. The example shows that they can still be adjusted to the four-beat pattern with thesis on the third beat by using shorter note values for the unaccented syllables. The diverse accentuation of the individual lines, however, results in four different patterns of note values within the same basic rhythm.

Because of the fluidity of its metrical structure the *settenario* line does not lend itself to the accompaniment of dance rhythms, which demand regularly recurring, identical patterns. With the exception of texts like *Accorta lusinghiera* that were probably written with regular accents expressly to suit the corrente rhythm, *settenario* stanzas are rarely used for dance songs.

On the other hand, the *settenario* line, precisely on account of its variability, is extremely well suited to the expression of strong and changing emotions; it is the favorite type of verse for the "affective" song that is to be sung in the free manner recommended by Caccini. Even in the setting of this kind of text, however, a few more or less stereotyped metric patterns are

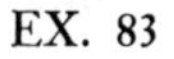
EX. 83

often used as a point of departure. In Brunelli's *Tu piangi al mio partire,* for instance (Ex. 84), we find the "lamento" pattern, of which Monteverdi's "Lasciatemi morire" from *Arianna* is a familiar example. Here the second syllable is lengthened as well as the last two, and the pattern is extended to fill six slow duple beats. The first two verses fall naturally into a $\frac{3}{2}$ meter. Later on in the song, however, the pattern is varied in many ways by prolonging whatever syllables require emphasis for the emotional expression of the text. The transcriber of this type of song should be prepared to change his time signatures and the lengths of his measures whenever this will help to clarify the accentuation of the individual line.

EX. 84

Summary

THE FOLLOWING TABLE summarizes the most common rhythmic patterns that are associated with each type of Italian verse in musical settings of the early seventeenth century. The notes on the upper line represent the note values assigned to each syllable of the verse. These are variable to the extent that the individual notes may be lengthened, shortened, or replaced by a melisma without departing from the metrical framework. The meter is shown in terms of modern time signatures and barlines. Two consecutive patterns are shown for each species of verse in order to clarify their relationship to the meter. Beats are represented by the lower notes and the arsic or thetic quality of each is indicated by the letters A and T.

TABLE IV: VERSE RHYTHMS

OTTONARIO RHYTHMS

Corrente rhythm · Four triple beats · See Examples 59 and 60, pp. 115f.

A A A T A A A T

Hemiola rhythm · Two triple + three duple beats · See Examples 61 and 62, p. 117.

A X A T T A X A T T

Six duple beats · See Examples 63–66, pp. 119f.

A X A A T T A X A A T T

Four fast duple beats · See Example 67, p. 120.

A A A T A A A T

Four slow duple beats · See Example 68, p. 121.

A A X T A A X T

Five slow duple beats · See Examples 69 and 70, pp. 121ff.

A A X T T A A X T T T

Gagliarda rhythm · Twelve duple beats on lower level · Four triple beats on upper level · See Example 71, p. 122.

AAA XAT AAA XAT AAA XAT AAA XAT

A T A T A T A T

QUINARIO RHYTHMS

Gagliarda rhythm · Six duple beats on lower level · Two triple beats on upper level · See Examples 72–74, pp. 123f.

AAA XAT AAA XAT

A T A T

Three duple beats starting with an upbeat · See Example 75, p. 124.

A X T A X T

Four duple beats starting with an upbeat · See Example 76, p. 125.

A X T T A X T T

SENARIO RHYTHMS

Corrente rhythm · Four triple beats to each pair of senarii · See Example 78, p. 125.

A T A T

Four duple beats starting with an upbeat · See Example 79, p. 126.

A A T T A A T T

SETTENARIO RHYTHMS

Corrente rhythm · Four triple beats · See Example 80, p. 127.

A A X T A A X T

Four duple beats starting with an upbeat · See Example 81, p. 127.

A A X T A A X T

Lamento rhythm · Six slow duple beats · See Example 84, p. 129.

A A X T T T A A X T T T

Four slow duple beats without upbeat · See Example 83, p. 129.

A A X T A A X T

Three triple beats starting with upbeat · See Example 82, p. 128.

A A T A A T

BIBLIOGRAPHY

Allegri, L. *Il Primo Libro delle Musiche*, Venice, 1618.
Apel, W. *The Notation of Polyphonic Music*, Cambridge, Mass., 1942.
———. "Anent a Ritornello in Monteverdi's *Orfeo*," *Musica Disciplina*, V (1951), 213.
Belli, D. *Arie a una e due voci per suonarsi col chitarrone*, Venice, 1616.
Benvenuti, G. Appendix to transcription of Monteverdi's *Orfeo*, 1609 edition.
Bononcini, G. M. *Musico Prattico*, Bologna, 1673.
Bottazzi, Fra B. *Choro et Organi. Primo Libro*, Venice, 1614.
Brunelli, A. *Regole utilissime per li scolari*, Florence, 1606.
———. *Scherzi, Arie, Canzonette, e Madrigali, Libro Primo*, Venice, 1612.
———. *Scherzi, Arie, Canzonette, e Madrigali, Libro Secondo*, Venice, 1614.
———. *Varii exercitii*, Florence, 1614.
———. *Scherzi, Arie, Canzonette, e Madrigali, Libro Terzo*, Venice, 1616.
———. *Fioretti spirituali*, Opus 15, Venice, 1626.
Bucchianti, P. *Arie, Scherzi, e Madrigali*, Venice, 1627.
Caccini, G. *Le Nuove Musiche*, Florence, 1602.
———. *Nuove Musiche e Nuova Maniera di Scriverle*, Florence, 1614.
Calestani, V. *Madrigali et Arie*, Venice, 1617.
Capece, A. *Il Secondo Libro de Madrigali et Arie*, Rome, 1625.
Carducci, G. *La poesia barbara*, Bologna, 1881.
———. "Dello svolgimento dell'ode in Italia," *Prose di Giosue Carducci*, Bologna, 1933.
Caroso, F. *Il Ballarino*, Venice, 1581.
———. *Nobiltà di Dame*, Venice, 1605.
Cavalliere, G. F. *Il scolare principiante*, Naples, 1634.
Cecchino, T. *Amorosi Concetti*, Venice, 1612.
Chilesotti, O. *Biblioteca di Rarità Musicali.*
Dolmetsch, M. *Dances of Spain and Italy*, London, 1954.
Falconieri, A. *Il 5to Libro delle Musiche*, Florence, 1619.
Fiorentino, E. "I ritmi della poesia Italiana sono quelli della musica," *Rivista Musicale Italiana*, XXIII, fasc. 2, 1916.
Fraccaroli, G. *D'una Teoria razionale di metrica italiana*, Turin, 1887.
Gagliano, G. B. da. *Varie Musiche. Libro Primo*, Venice, 1623.
Gagliano, M. da. *Musiche*, Venice, 1615.
Gandini, S. *Correnti et Balletti alla Francese et all'Italiana*, Venice, 1655.
Leonetti, P. *Storia della tecnica del verso italiano*, Rome, 1933.

Magri, D. *Armoniosi Accenti*, Turin, 1956.

Mendel, A. "A Brief Note on Triple Proportions in Schütz," *The Musical Quarterly*, XLVI (1960), 67.

Monteverdi, C. *Incoronazione di Poppea*, facs. of MS. It. Cl. 4 N. 439 in Bibl. Naz. di S. Marco. Ed. Benvenuti, Milan, 1938

Morley, T. *Plaine and Easie Introduction to Practical Musicke*. London, 1597.

Murari, R. *Ritmica e metrica razionale italiana*, Milan, 1900.

Negri, C. *Nuovi Inventioni di Balli*, Milan, 1604.

Noske, F. "Two Problems in Seventeenth Century Notation," *Acta Musicologica*, XVII, fasc. III–IV (1955).

Olifante, G. B. "Trattato Brevissimo intorno alle Proportioni cantabile," in Rodio, R. *Regole di Musica*, Naples, 1608 (dated 1611).

d'Ovidio, Fr. *Versificazione Romanza*, Naples, 1932.

Pace, P. *Primo Libro de Madrigali*, Venice, 1613.

Penna, L. *Li primi albori musicali*, Bologna, 1672.

Picerli, S. *Specchio . . . di Musica*, Vol. I, Naples, 1630.

Pisa, A. *Battuta della musica dichiarata*, Rome, 1611.

Peri, J. *Le Musiche di Jacopo Peri*, Florence, 1600.

________. *Varie Musiche*, Florence, 1609.

Pernicone, V. *Storia e svolgimento della metrica*, Milan, 1948.

Pesenti, M. *Il Primo Libro delle Corrente per sonar nel clavicembalo*, Venice, 1635.

________. *Il Quarto Libro de Madrigali*, Venice, 1638.

Porta, H. *Hore di Recreatione Musicale*, Venice, 1612.

Rasi, Fr. *Madrigali di diversi autori*, Florence, 1610.

Rontani, R. *Le Varie Musiche*, Florence, 1614.

Rossi, P. *Metrica italiana e classica*, Milan, 1949.

Sachs, C. *World History of the Dance*, New York, 1937.

Sab[b]atini, P. P. *Il Sesto. Opera Ottava*, Rome, 1628.

Sances, G. F. *Cantade a voce sola*, Venice, 1633.

Saracini, C. *Le Seconde Musiche*, Venice, 1633.

Scaletta, H. *Scala di Musica corretta*, Milan, 1657.

Strata, G. B. *Arie di musica*, Genoa, 1610.

Strunk, O. *Source Readings in Music History*, New York, 1950.

Tacchinardi, A. *Ritmica musicale*, 2nd ed. Milan, 1926.

Tacone, G. *Armonicus Parnassus*, Rome, 1628.

Tani, G. "Le comte d'Aglie et le Ballet de Cour en Italie," *Les Fêtes de la Renaissance*, Paris, 1956.

Torre, P. P. *Primo Libro delle Canzonette*, Venice, 1622.

Visconti, D. *Il Primo Libro di Arie*, Venice, 1616.

Vitali, F. *Musiche a due, tre e sei voci*, Florence, 1617.

Westphal, R. *Die Fragmente und Lehrsätze der griechischen Rythmiker*, 1861.

Williams, C. D., Abdy. *The Aristoxenian Theory of Musical Rhythm*, Cambridge, 1911.

Zambaldi, F. *Il ritmo dei versi*, Turin, 1882.

Zan[n]etti, G. *Il scolaro*, Milan, 1645.

ANTHOLOGY OF ITALIAN SONGS AND DANCES

ANTHOLOGY OF ITALIAN SONGS AND DANCES

Notes on the Transcriptions

SOURCES. The sources upon which these transcriptions are based will be found among those listed on page 14f. of Chapter I of this book. The method of transcription follows the principles outlined in that Chapter, including an attempt to clarify the rhythmic structure of the music through its placement on the page.

MEASURE. The time signatures and note values are original except where the contrary is indicated by an incipit in the original notation. The original barlines, if any, are marked by a dash above the staff. In pieces originally bearing the signature C, it has been necessary to increase some measures by one or more beats to make the phrasing of the music clear. In these cases a [$\frac{3}{2}$] or [$\frac{4}{2}$] has been added in brackets above the voice part, but the value of the half note remains constant. The note values of pieces originally signed C $\frac{6}{4}$ are reduced in our transcription to $\frac{6}{8}$ or [$\frac{6}{8}$ $\frac{3}{4}$]. Again the note values are constant. Where there is a change of meter in the course of a piece small notes above the voice part [♩. = ♩] show the equivalence of the note values under the two signs.

The layout of the music on the page is designed to show its relationship to the poetry. Consequently, measures are often broken off at the end of a line and concluded on the next line.

ACCIDENTALS. Redundant accidentals have been suppressed. Accidentals in brackets are editorial.

ACCOMPANIMENTS. Figured basses are original, but figures that were originally placed between the staves have been placed below the bass line. Realizations of the figured basses are by the present author.

Ritornelli. The instrumental *ritornelli* (postludes or interludes to be played between the stanzas) were originally written as a single melodic line and intended to be performed by a violin, recorder, or other melodic instrument. When such instruments are used the harmony should be completed by the accompanist at the keyboard; in some cases a blank staff has been left for the accompanist to fill in. Accompanists who desire to play the melodies of the *ritornelli* at the keyboard should include only as much of the harmony as is easily feasible. A basic accompaniment has sometimes been provided on the same staff as the *ritornello*.

Literary Texts. The original spelling has been preserved, even where it is erratic or incorrect according to modern standards. Nor has punctuation been added, although it is almost totally absent in the original sources. The original capitalization and the layout on the page indicate the length of the verse lines; any further interpretation has been left to the individual performer.

Calligraphy and layout by Erich Schwandt.

SONGS
IN OTTONARIO METER

DI QUEL NUDO PARGOLETTO

Ballo Grave

Scherzi, Canzonetti e Madrigali. Libro Terzo, 1616 ANTONIO BRUNELLI

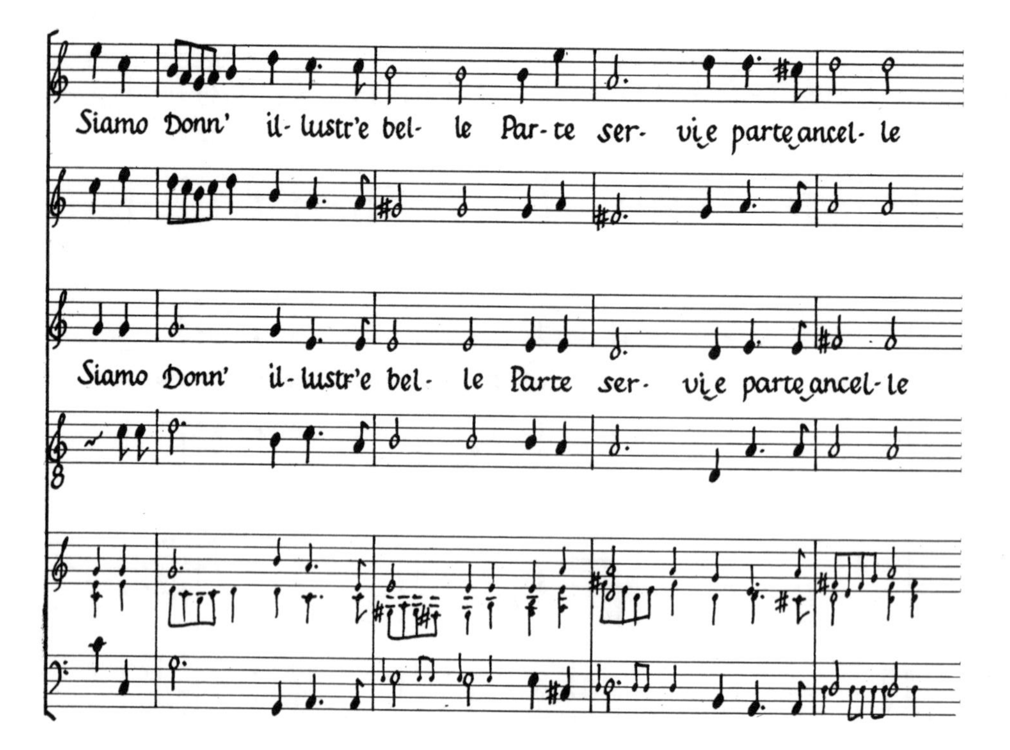
Siamo Donn' il- lustr'e bel- le Par- te ser- vi e parte ancel- le
Siamo Donn' il- lustr'e bel- le Parte ser- vi e parte ancel- le

Parte ser- vi e parte ancel- le
Par- te ser- vi e parte ancel- le

Ritornello

ALLE PIAGGE ALME

Part II, as a *Gagliarda*

In qual par- te Amor soggior- na Et a noi per- che non tor- na
In qual par- te Amor soggior- na Et a noi per- che non tor- na

Et a noi perche non tor- na
Et a noi perche non tor- na

Ritornello

NELLE VAGHE TRECE

Part III, as a *Corrente*

1. Nel- le vaghe tre- ce bion-de Di voi Donn' e nel bel vol- to

2. Tra i vermigli e bian-chi fio- ri Del- le guance i lac- ci ten- de

3. Già scoper- bo non ap-prez- za Pa- so o Ci- pri e del suo re- gno

4. Ma s'ei fa ne vostri aspet- ti Sol pa-le- si i van- ti suo- i

1. Tut- to lie- to s'e rac-col- to Ne vostr'oc-chi si nascon- de

2. A ve- dergli al-letta e pren- de Al- let- tan- do mil- le co- ri

3. Sti- ma seggio alte- ro e de- gno Donne sol vostra bel-lez- za

4. Voi fa-re- te A-more e no- i A servi- re Amore e- let- ti

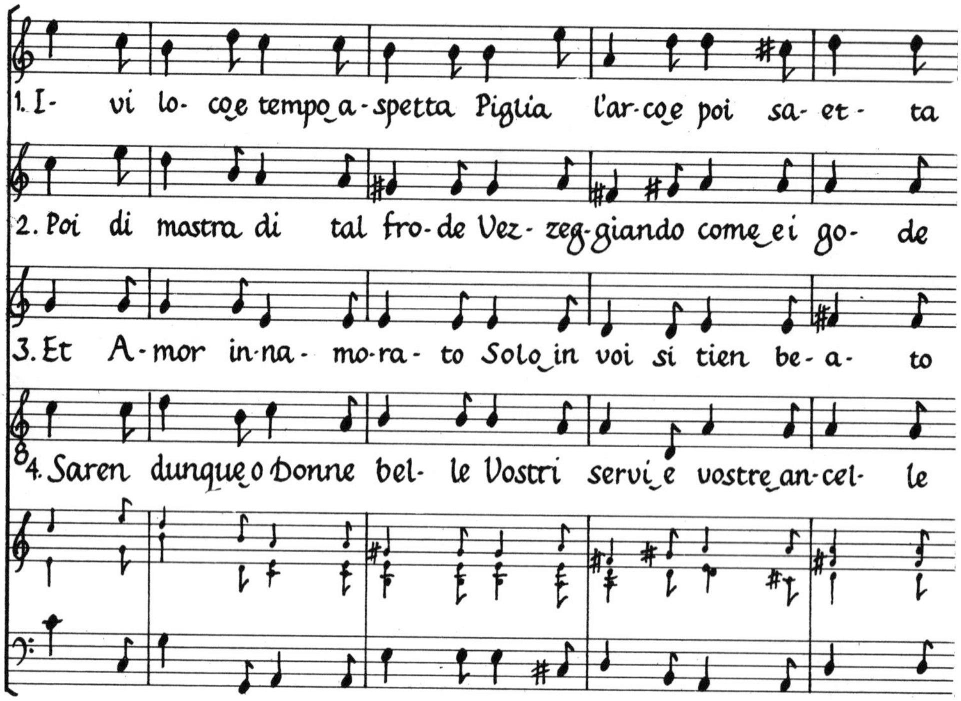

1. I- vi lo- co e tempo a-spetta Piglia l'ar-co e poi sa-et- ta

2. Poi di mastra di tal fro-de Vez- zeg-giando come ei go- de

3. Et A-mor in-na- mo-ra- to Solo in voi si tien be- a- to

4. Saren dunque o Donne bel- le Vostri servi e vostre an-cel- le

1. Piglia l'ar-co e poi sa- et- ta

2. Vez-zeg-giando come ei go- de

3. Solo in voi si tien be- a- to

4. Vostri servi e vostre an-cel- le.

Ritornello

NON HA'L CIEL COTANTI LUMI

MS Florence B. N. *Magl. IX, 66*

GIULIO CACCINI

Cor gentil che s'in- namo ra

NON HA'L CIEL COTANTI LUMI

(Embellished version)

Nuove Musiche e nuova maniera di scriverla, 1614 GIULIO CACCINI

2

Neve al sol e nebbia al vento
E d'Amor gioia e contento
Degli affanni e delle pene
Ahi che 'l fin già mai non viene
Giel' di morte estingue ardore
Ch' in van alma accende Amore

3

Ben soll' io che 'l morir solo
Può dar fine al mio gran duolo
Ne di voi gia mi dogl' io
Del mio stato acerbo e rio
Solo Amor tiranno accuso
Occi belli e voi ne scuso

4

Penar' lungo e gioir corto
Morir' vivo e viver' morto
Spem' incerta e van' desire
Merce poca à gran languire
Falsi risi e veri pianti
È la vita degli amanti

TEXT BY OTTAVIO RINUCCINI

PASTORELLA OVE TI ASCONDI

Il Primo Libra di Arie, 1616 DOMENICO VISCONTI

2

Se tu parti e chi mi aita
Se t'en vai chi mi consola
Che farà della mia vita
Senza te misera e sola
Non partire o Filli aspetta
Non fuggiti con tanta fretta

3

Pria che parta ohimè rimira
Queste lacrime cocenti
Vede il cor ch'a morte spira
Senza gl'occhi tuoi lucenti
Pastorella ferma il piede
Questa sia la mia mercede

4

Ma tu ingrata a me t'en fuggi
Ne mai ascolti ò mi consoli
Sai ben tu che mi distruggi
Col fuggire e pur t'en voli
Dimmi almeno o Filli adio
Moria poi lieto il cor mio

PASTORELLA OVE TI ASCONDI

Musiche a una e due voci. Libro Secondo, 1618 — FILIPPO VITALI

QUI VEDRÒ QUEL CHIARO SOLE

Quarto Libro di Madrigali, 1638 MARTINO PESENTI

Qui ve-drò quel chiaro so-le Che miei dì suol far se- re-ni

E tra questi colli a- me-ni non sa-rà chi me l'i- mo-le

non sa- rà non sa- rà non sa- rà chi me imo- le

Qui ve-drò quel chiaro sole qui ve-dro qui ve- dro

Ritornello Primo

Vl. 1°, 2°

SONGS
IN SETTENARIO METER

IO PUR DEGGIO PARTIRE

as a *Gagliarda*

Madrigali et Arie Per sonare et cantare, 1617 VINCENZO CALESTANI

In Gagliarda

2

O duol fammi di sasso
Pria che si movi il piè
Morte mi tronchi il passo
Se far mi vuol mercè

3

Ahimè di che ragiono
Se già m'ha spento il duol
E come ombra non sono
Se più non vedo il sol

4

E pur la doglia sento
D'un immortal venen
E qual saria il tormento
Se'l core io havessi in sen

5

Cor mio dovè t'arresti
Et io dovè me'n vò
Leggiadri occhi celesti
Quando vi rivedrò

6

S'io v'amo e s'io v'adoro
S'allo la terra e'l ciel
E pur vi lascio e moro
O mio destin crudel

7

Deh perchè la mia morte
Almen costei non sà
Perche della mia sorte
Non sente almen pietà

8

Eh Dio s'udir potessi
Il suon di miei sospir
S'el mio pensier vedessi
Ahi ch'io no'l posso dir.

ACCORTA LUSINGHIERA

the same as a *Corrente*

Madrigali et Arie Per sonare et cantare, 1617 VINCENZO CALESTANI

La sopradetta in Corrente con altre parole

2

Negar negar non puoi
Ahi cruda ahi disleal
Colpo de gl'occhi tuoi
La mia piaga mortal

3

Che nella fronte scritto
De l'empia il nome sta
De l'empia che trasfitto
Si fieramente m'ha

4

Vedi come t'inganni
Ch'io mi finga i martir
Ch'io non sostenga affanni
Ch'io falseggi i sospir

5

In pianti mi distillo
Disciolto ai lumi il fren'
Di fuori ardo e sfavillo
Colmo di fiamme il sen'

6

Da mè da mè il diletto
Ha preso lunge il vol
E nel piagato petto
Tormento albergar' sol

7

E se la tua bellezza
Mi tien lasso prigion'
Così la tua fierezza
E del mio duol cagion'

NON HAVEA FEBO ANCORA

Scherzi, Arie, Canzonette e Madrigali. Libro Secondo, 1614 ANTONIO BRUNELLI

2

Su 'l pallidetto volto
Scorgeari il suo dolor
Spesso le venia sciolto
Un gran sospir dal cor
Miserell', etc.

3

Si calpestando i fiori
Errava hor quà e là
Ei sua perduti amori
Così piangendo và
Miserell', etc.

4

Amor diceva e 'l piè
Mirando il ciel fermò
Dove dove è la fè
Ch' il traditor giurò
Miserell', etc.

5

Se 'l ciglio ha più sereno
Colei che 'l mio non è
Gia non gli albergo in seno
Amor si nobil fè
Miserell', etc.

6

Fa ch' ei riorni mio
Amor com' ei pur sù
O tu m'ancidi ch' io
Non mi tormenti più
Miserell', etc.

7

Ne mai più dolci baci
Da quella bocca havrò
Ne più soave ai taci
Taci che troppo il sò
Miserell', etc.

8

Poiche di lui mi struggo
Dove stima non fa
Che si che si ch' io 'l fuggo
Ch' ancor mi preghera
Miserell', etc.

9

Si tra sdegnosi pianti
Sfogava il suo dolor
Si de gentil amanti
Misto è coglielo Amor
Miserell', etc.

PASTOR' LEVATE SU

Musiche a una, due e tre voci, 1615 MARCO DA GAGLIANO

Par- go- letto gen- til
Quel che fabri-co 'l Ciel
Nu- do sul l'a- spro fien
Fra due giumen-ti stà
Deh chi mirar sostien l'e- ter- ne sua bel- tà

Non più tar-dar sù Lie-ti mo-ve-te il piè
Ad ado-rar Gie-sù

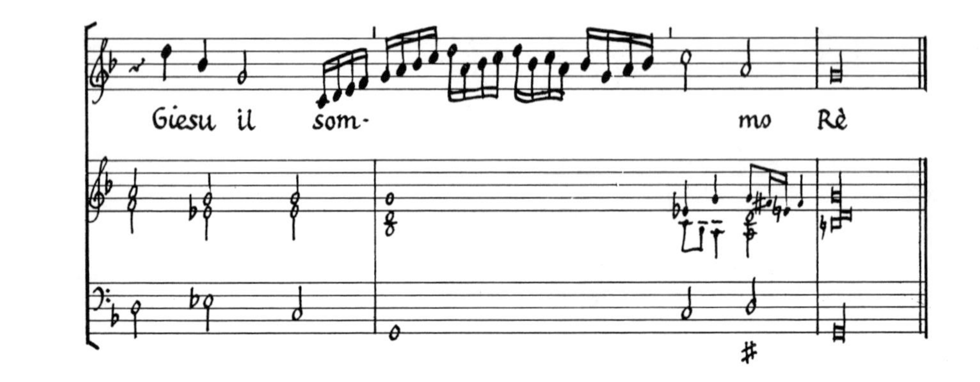
Giesu il som- mo Rè

SONGS
IN QUINARIO METER

NON VUOI CH'IO T'AMI

Il Primo Libro di Arie, 1616 DOMENICO VISCONTI

2

Se mi disprezzi
Mi fuggirò
Nè mai per vezzi
Ritornerò
E tu crudele
E l'infidele
Ogn' hor detta sarai
Guarda che fai

3

S' à gioco prendi
La mia gran fè
In vano attendi
Ch' arda per te
E tu incostante
La non amante
Ogn' hor detta sarai
Guarda che fai

4

S' il mio dolore
Gioir ti fà
E in me l'ardore
Si spegnierà
E tu la cruda
Di pietà ignuda
Ogn' hor detta sarai
Guarda che fai

5

S' in te pietade
Non troverò
La tua beltade
Non seguirò
E tu l'altera
E la severa
Ogn' hor detta sarai
Guarda che fai

6

Ma se 'l tuo lume
Dolce vedrò
Te quasi Nume
Adorerò
E tu pietosa
E l'amorosa
Ogn' hor detta sarai
Guarda che fai

AH, LADRA D'AMORE

Varie Musiche. Libro Primo, 1623

GIOVAN BATISTA DE GAGLIANO

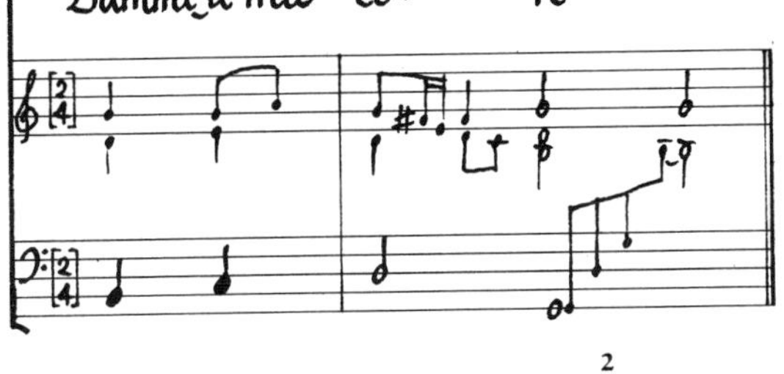

Ah Traditorella
A me rubella
Dhe gira homai
Quei dolce rai
Vedi ch' io moro
Per grave martoro
Porgi mi aita
Filli mia vita
Ah Ladra d'Amore
Dammi il mio core

SONGS IN SENARIO METER

GIOITE GIOITE

Varie Musiche. Libro Primo, 1623 GIOVAN BATISTA DE GAGLIANO

2

Ridete ridete
Pupille vitali
Mirat' e credete
Mia pene mortali
Per tanti mie mali
S'accresca il contento
Se preme il mio seno
So ver chio tormento

3

Godete godete
Dell'empia mia sorte
Se l'ora scorgete
Vicina di morte
Fallaci mia scorte
Pur liete vi miro
Ne spera il desio
Sù l'ultimo a Dio
Chi breve sospiro

4

Scherzate scherzate
Per somma dolcezza
Negate pietate
Crescete fierezza
Da cruda bellezza
L'afflitta mia vita
Per lieve mercede
Un sguardo sol chiede
Per ultima aita

FUGGI FUGGI FUGGI DA QUESTO CIELO

MS *Barbera*, Conservatorio L. Cherubini, Florence — Giuseppino del Biabo

2

Vieni vieni candida vien vermiglia
Tu del mondo sei maraviglia
Tu nemica d'amare noie
Dà ad anima delle gioie
Messaggiera
Per primavera
Tu sei del' anno la giovinezza
Tu del mondo sei la vaghezza

3

Vieni vieni vieni leggiadra e vaga
Primavera d'amor presaga
Odi Zeffiro che t'invita
E la terra col ciel marita
Al suo raggio
Venga maggio
Pieno il grembo di bei fioretti
Vien sù l'ali dhe Zeffiretti

TU PIANGI AL MIO PARTIRE

Scherzi, Arie, Canzonetti e Madrigali. Libro Terzo, 1616 ANTONIO BRUNELLI

2

Deh piangi e i lumi gira
A me che piango e moro
S'io t'amo e s'io t'adoro
Nel mio partir rimira
Senti come sospira
Questo mio cor deh senti
Questi voci dolenti
E qual governo fa di
me 'l duol interno

3

Perder l'amor la vita
Predo di nemico empio
Per me sia lieve scempio
Sia lieve ogni ferita
Mandate far partita
E troppo audace volo
A ch'a pensarvi solo
E cangio il pelo e nelle
fiamme gelo

4

Partita aspra e funesta
Io di te priva e cieco
Che bene havrò più meco
Che piu sperar me resta?
Altri gioisca in festa?
Che giunto e 'l morir mio
A Dio mio bene à Dio
Mia fè pregiate e chi
v'adora amate

INDEX

INDEX

INDEX ENTRIES in italics indicate the presence of a musical example from the work in question. The complete works included in the Anthology are not listed in the index.